# PEOPLE AT WORK

## THE ART OF LIVING AND SURVIVING

TEXT AND PHOTOGRAPHS

# IAGO CORAZZA AND GRETA ROPA

PROJECT EDITOR
VALERIA MANFERTO DE FABIANIS

GRAPHIC DESIGN
PAOLA PIACCO

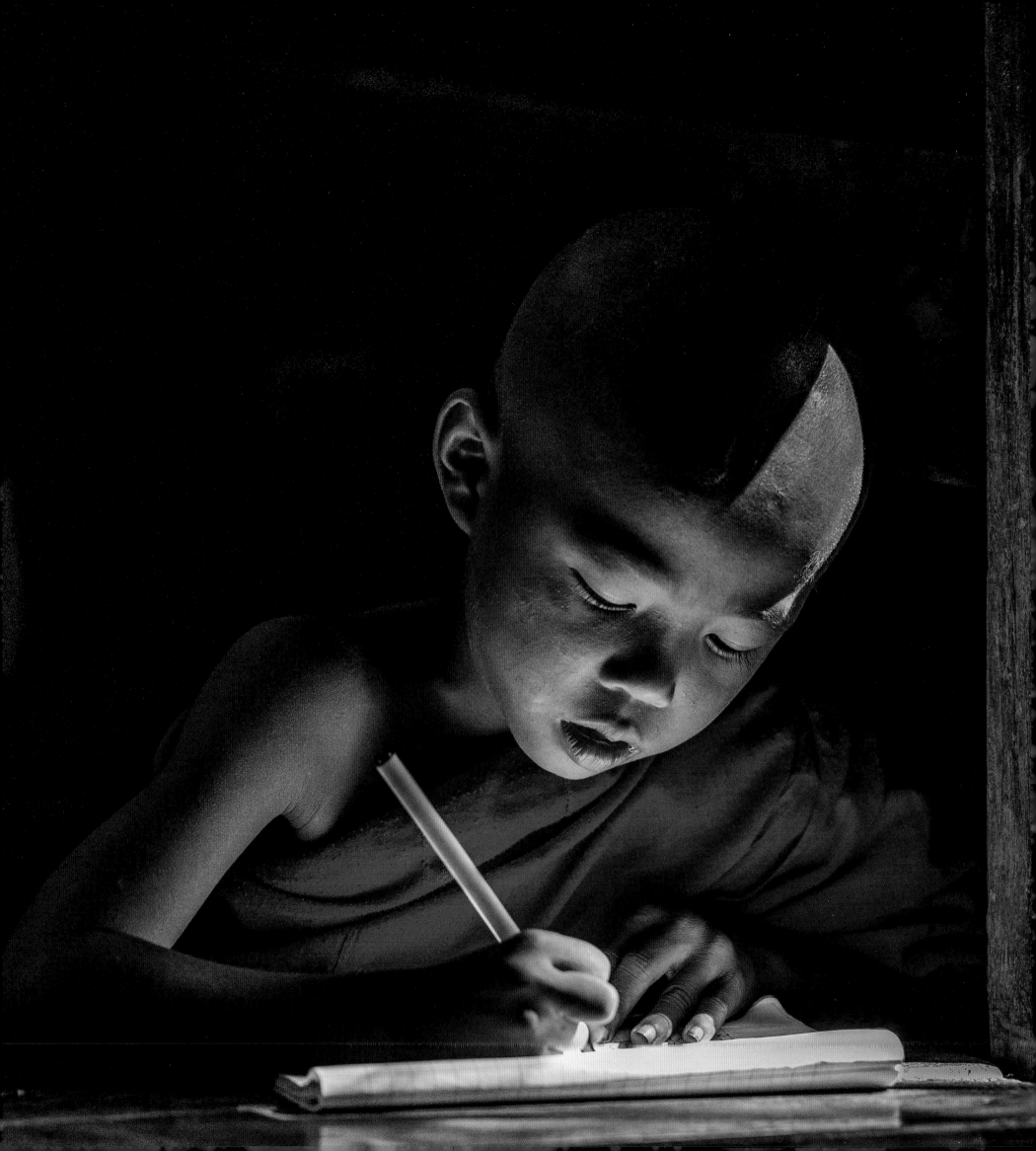

# Contents

# Foreword

Many a time during our travels we interrupted our walk or ride and cut short our conversation because we were surprised and attracted by the types of activity and work we noticed. Like a magnet, a center of gravity, or an occult power, this phenomenon is an expression of human civilization, evolution, and culture. We have always observed it with a view to, in some way, absorbing its skill, its value and its secrets merely by capturing it with our cameras. What this activity was mattered very little, provided it stemmed from human industry through the movement of hands and arms, or through the effort made to realize ideas, dreams and projects. Man and his work have always attracted our attention, especially the type that is part of what we call the *informal economy*. Wherever there is a world made up of laws, regulations, acquired rights and respected duties or class and corporate consciousness, there is also another world consisting of improvisation, self-sufficiency, conquest and 'unofficial' activity. We have always observed, avidly, the world of the informal from a privileged standpoint and with a solid history of a long and difficult course of sacrifice both of human lives and of social changes. It is almost as if it were an ideal place in which to search for traces of something lost, perhaps driven by the need to regain the human space and dimension that have been sacrificed, inevitably, for the sake of tutelage, progress or a new civilization. And, it is precisely in these areas of activity – which are often illegal and unacknowledged – that we have often portrayed the marvel of man and his ability to find solutions to problems and needs of every kind. Such solutions have sometimes come about because of some extemporaneous ingenuity that has not survived in our modern world or in the impersonal and anonymous names given to categories of work for purely bureaucratic or administrative purposes. The occupations we have captured have the same DNA, so to speak, as our present-day ones, but these latter have often changed so much that they have become unrecognizable, sometimes have new names, and their purpose and social utility have often gone by the wayside.

So here we are, survivors of an economic boom, castaways of a New Economy, looking back at a world that still exists. The lights, now LED-based, at an improvised evening market in Benin. A traditional physician who operates in the street and butchers in China. A barber who cuts hair on the steps of Ghats in India. A farmer who harvests taro in Oceania. What do the images of these working people – drawn from our repertoire of experience and nostalgia and from our photographic archives – have in common? Perhaps it is the fact that they have not been standardized or, perhaps because they are often in the most remote places on Earth, that they have been bypassed by the Western business model. Perhaps what they have in common is the human reaction of individuals who still see to the basic needs and survival of their families. They may only represent the last possible stage of the absence of the negative effects that money has on people, that favorable positions have on the individual and that power has on the ultimate goal. Yet, we are aware that this continuous activity, which keeps the immense sea of informal work moving, constitutes the structural framework of the entire labor market. And, although it is the only opportunity that this slice of humanity has to participate in the global market, this work, which avoids and eschews all norms and regulations, is a metaphor for inequality and a generator of alternative strategies of survival and development in forms that will not disappear as quickly as economists had initially supposed. We also know how much the informal economy, given its heterogeneous character, creates job insecurity and deprives governments of resources. On the other hand, especially at critical times, it is the sector that suffers the worst repercussions, such as sudden salary cuts and longer working hours, which arise in order for that market to survive. What attracts us in these areas is the spectacle of this great mass of humanity that expresses itself, works, produces and, above all, acts. We may have concentrated our attention so much on this symbolic area of working procedure because, as reporters, travelers and human beings, we are more at ease in a world managed with the approximation of the informal, where what is uncertain is always possible, where situations often depend on other situations and where things may still happen. Of course, we also hope for a world of work consisting of respected rights, justice, constant improvement in working conditions for every individual and compatible productivity, awareness and fulfillment. In other words, we want the security and advantages of the formal as well as the hope and humanity so characteristic of the informal. Therefore, we will continue to imagine a utopia with norms created by men for men, a world whose ultimate aim is not financial gain but human fulfillment. In short, we will continue to work, with hope in the future of a New Human Economy.

# ntroduction

After so many years of traveling the world, meeting new people, who are often very different from us, there is a question that is especially disturbing and that we always hope will not be the first one we will be asked: "So, what line of work are you in?" The difficulty in answering this eternal question lies in our personal lifestyle choice, always on the move among the vicissitudes of the system, drifting between photojournalism, anthropology, trips of exploration and discovery, and the simple curiosity of the next-door neighbor. It is no easy task to explain to a farmer on the Trobriand Islands that the photos we take and the words we jot down so enthusiastically in our notebook are an integral part of our work. Or that the very experiences we are now having thanks to his help and the opportunity to spend precious time among his community, will allow us, indirectly, to give lectures, write a book or an article, and put at the disposal of our readers and photography students a precious and heartfelt observation of a rare and different culture. Last but not least, these experiences in the field will, inevitably, change our view of life. A question often asked is: "But is this really an occupation in your country?" These considerations struck us immediately and seemed anything but ingenuous. Therefore, on many occasions during our travels we found it difficult to explain our profession and hoped that there would be at least one physician, or else someone who had a universally 'acceptable' job, among friends and fellow adventurers. The work undertaken by citizens of the northern hemisphere often stems from an extremely stratified, specialized and complex society that consumes services more than it consumes products. It contracts out services, conceives them and creates a need for them. The consumer is sometimes 'generated' after the product is commercialized, in conformity with a form of market strategy. So we spent hours lying on a banana-leaf mat describing the occupations of women in our society to some curious farmers in Vanuatu, or trying to explain to a group of untouchables in India, whose job was to sort the bones of corpses, what a product manager does on a normal workday. In truth, describing our professions in front of the pitiless mirror of that part of the world was one of the most interesting anthropological exercises we have had occasion to carry out recently. Globalization has certainly guaranteed a greater degree of democracy in the media, but, at the same time, it has created an increasingly clear-cut division between the occupations that are still based on forms *doing and acting*, and those based on *being*. Almost all of our acquaintances are consultants, managers, computer technicians and trainers, or else 'are in the communication sector', while our photographic subjects are taxi drivers, tanners, farmers, carpenters and blacksmiths, and a mere photograph of their hands is often enough to give an indication of their line of work. We struggled to explain to them precisely what our skills are, simply because most of us were unable to do anything except analyze, choose, manage, mediate, and coordinate, and we often justified this by calling it *being*, which identifies a role but is certainly not a practical skill. Hence, the working people documented in this book ended up being considered almost magicians by us

Westerners, we who are theoretical and hyper-specialized. Their comments, their irony, the filter of their personality, all restored a vision of ourselves and of the most authentic, living world, the fruit of practical and operative intelligence. This is why we are so fond of these world workers, because in our opinion they are the most generous and faithful examples of their societies. Obviously, a vendor in a marketplace is not only a vendor. The way he offers his merchandise, the products he chooses, how he occupies the space and manages money, the relationship he has with his clients – all provide an absolutely faithful account of the society he lives in. Again, only among the occupations in the southern hemisphere have we noticed a proliferation of flexibility, approximation, common sense and humanity. The people who work through action always favor humans over regulations, laws, and 'the system'. Thus, their gestures have so often led us to fantasize about what our profession would be like in another life or another place. We have spied on lives that seemed to be much more in a human dimension, certainly more fatiguing but less oppressive than life in our world. Only to discover, however, that each of these workers, industrious creators of merchandise that is also earmarked for the rest of the world, almost always dreams of a future as a product manager for himself and his children. After pondering silently over some of our replies to his questions, an elderly man from Papua New Guinea asked us, with sincere curiosity and wholly without any irony: "So, in the end, what is it you know how to do?" We thought about this for a little, which in itself was indicative. Then we answered that perhaps the only thing we really knew how to do was observe and be amazed. The old man had a good belly laugh and, pouring some more *kava*, considered the beverage of sincerity, declared that that was the best job he had ever heard of.

2   The skilled hands of this craftsman accompany a multi-colored fabric that will become a stole or perhaps a sari. Located on the doorstep of the house, he uses only the shelf of his faithful old sewing machine.

4   In Myanmar, it is customary for every young person to pass a period of time as a novice in a monastery at some point between the ages of seven and twenty. This important passage in life is a source of pride both for individuals and for the whole family.

6-7   The Assam is one of the most fertile and climatically suitable zones for the cultivation of high quality tea. Here, plantations are vast and cover entire hills and valleys, attracting seasonal workers who are predominantly women.

14-15   In the past, Gopalpur-on-the-Sea was an important Indian port town. Today the situation has changed, but you can still see many fishermen operating with traditional boats and methods.

# People at Work

By now everyone is well aware of the progressive and inexorable marginalization of Europe and North America within the context of the global economy. The old processes of accumulation and economic development, in line with traditional geo-political principles, have been in a profound crisis since the 1980s. On the other side of the coin is the obvious central role played by the economic growth in Asia, further favored by the latest major phase of technological innovation, which is connected to the New Economy. However, what we often fail to grasp is the complex dynamic that regulates the evolution of the world of work. One needn't be an expert in economics to note the day-by-day transformation in the complex fabric of international economic relations, which have recently become intertwined and fused, creating a kind of global destiny that we all depend upon. We often remark on how the economic world has changed, and the labor market is undoubtedly the most faithful indication of this profound social change.

Yet, despite the many achievements and the indisputable improvements in overall living conditions, to some extent we have all perceived that, by now, the idyll of the delicate relationship between humanity and work has fallen apart. We often have the sensation that this lost dignity can not be regained, that the aura of sacredness once attributed to work has lost some of its sheen, that the rights earned by workers have been periodically nullified. This perception recently arose with the formation of the present global productive system, which has neutralized – and not very gradually, let it be said – the old configuration of nation-states or alliances of countries, understood as blocs that are more or less developed and organized: the First, Second, Third and Fourth Worlds. Such subdivision, which once belonged to a more traditional economy, one that was more a part of a mindset of exchange between raw materials and finished products, has created a cultural heritage that must now, necessarily, be reconsidered and revised, since it is no longer pertinent to present-day reality.

The economic world, and thus the world of work, is now too complex to be reduced to the categories of the haves and have-nots, as conceived by the American scholar Harris. Rather, contemporary economists must agree on a world view that embraces the substantial dualism of *nucleus* and *periphery*, not so much as a geographic concept as a social relationship. Recently, emphasis has been placed on the relationship among groups belonging to the same social class – for example the middle class or the world's working class. Consequently, today, worldwide class politics are viewed in an utterly different way, depending on whether one is dealing with nuclei or peripheries. So, we have multinational corporations and the élite of the Third World on the same level, so to speak, connected perhaps by their common exploitation of workers or by the harm they cause to the environment, unfortunately on a worldwide scale.

Specifically, recent decades have witnessed the relocation of industrial activity from the more developed nations to the poorer countries and a general transfer of capital to financial activities. All this has greatly altered the organization of the global labor market, and jobs that once constituted a guarantee, a source of security and a value for our society, have undergone a genetic transformation, so to speak, as has the relationship with employers and entrepreneurs that for centuries regulated and influenced the welfare state. At the present time, leaving aside the location, and except for some areas that are wholly or partly removed from this context, employers in fact are nothing more or less than large groups with large amounts of capital at their disposal that they administer at a global level. Their policy often consists of comparing the earnings and the capital invested, thus following the logic of maximum profit, organizing and influencing the entire world. This dynamic has, undoubtedly, made the world of work much more complex and perhaps somewhat more alien to workers, although it must be said that the Establishment has always existed and has always wielded power, influencing society and politics. Yet economists agree, for example, that the overall number of poor people in the world has decreased. But it is equally true that most of these people are now concentrated in countries that have average wages and that are enjoying rapid economic growth, such as the 'Asian Tigers' China and India. And these are precisely the nations that have the greatest social and economic disparity and are witnessing the development of a large *informal economy* network, with its lack of guarantees and rights, and its inadequate pay. This sector is a kind of economic-social magma: work that is unregulated, thus not officially registered or recognized and is not taxed. Furthermore, in many countries, this condition is the rule rather than the exception, an integral part of everyday life, the only possible way for everyone to have a job. On the other hand, in what was once called the First World, this situation is gradually disappearing, so that we must struggle with the difficulty in understanding this complex new economy, as well as the new approach to work that it entails. Thus, the model of development that now prevails associates economic growth with greater domestic inequality as well as a reduction of extreme poverty in developing countries. However, this does not solve the problem of these countries' vulnerability. In any case, the benchmark of the great economic and social question is still the jobs front. Work is still the key not only to the fulfillment of the individual, but also to the development of cohesive and hence functioning, societies. Therefore, the photographs in this book are a tribute to all the facets of the concept of work, especially those that sustain the informal economy, which to this day may be the economy that most exemplifies man and which provides interesting food for thought concerning the ideal we should try to attain.

# With the Head

chapter 1

Over the years, we have been able to observe the various means of realizing an occupation. More than the 'instruments' used in what we call informal work, what fascinated us most were the different ways in which this latter is manifested and develops, generating an amazing 'mosaic' of activity that is subject to continuous change. For the most part, during this journey we photographed work performed mainly with the arms, the legs and the hands. Other occupations were based more upon experience or drew inspiration directly from creativity. Consequently, having been totally won over by an experience that offered so much beauty, we tried to subdivide this human form of work, which is the driving force of our world. In so doing, well aware that it would be impossible to draw up an 'official' or traditional ranking, we chose only one major 'ingredient' among the many in this 'recipe'. Rather than dwell on the aim of each occupation, we set out to group the many activities according to their affinity with energy, the emotions they conveyed, and the strong impact made upon us when we observed it carefully. From what can be judged by what we saw and what our cameras registered, the dominant influence in the world of informal work is its energy and, consequently, we have singled out the categories as if they were parts or attitudes of the human body. And, in fact, the first subdivision includes work carried out with the energy stemming from the head and the intellect. These are occupations that, despite their occasional condition of absolute improvisation or the fact that they are influenced by cultural or environmental factors, require planning, mental activity, specific formation, and a particular inclination. In ancient times, the head was considered the seat of the soul, the noble temple of that mystery known as man. Therefore, we will begin our photographic account with the head, although very soon we will discover that the soul of human action can be found in the most diverse of places.

# Teachers

ASIDES FROM BEING A JOB, TEACHING IS WITHOUT
A DOUBT A PROFESSION OF UNQUESTIONED SOCIAL VALUE.
IN PRACTICE, THE ACTUAL WORK INVOLVED IS VERY LITTLE
COMPARED TO THE RESPONSIBILITY AND EMOTIONAL
INVESTMENT REQUIRED TO BE A GOOD TEACHER.
IF WE ALSO CONSIDER THE AVAILABLE RESOURCES,
WHICH ARE NEVER ENOUGH ALMOST EVERYWHERE
IN THE WORLD, THE VALUE OF THIS CHOICE STANDS OUT
EVEN MORE. TEACHERS ARE OFTEN DEEMED MORAL
REFERENCE POINTS, LOCAL AUTHORITIES WHERE THERE IS
NO ALTERNATIVE, IMPORTANT EDUCATIONAL NUCLEI OUTSIDE
THE FAMILY, AND IN EVERY CORNER OF THE WORLD
THEY ARE PLANTING SEEDS OF KNOWLEDGE.
THEY ARE ALMOST ALWAYS UNITED BY AN INVISIBLE
YET LUMINESCENT THREAD OF PASSION AND THE ABILITY
TO GET PERSONALLY INVOLVED.

ba    be    bi    bo    bu

cha    che    chi    chu    chu

da    de    di    do    du

fa    fe    fi    fo    fu

ga    ge    gi    go    gu

500ml

ON (Pty) Ltd.

MOJA    MBILI    TATU

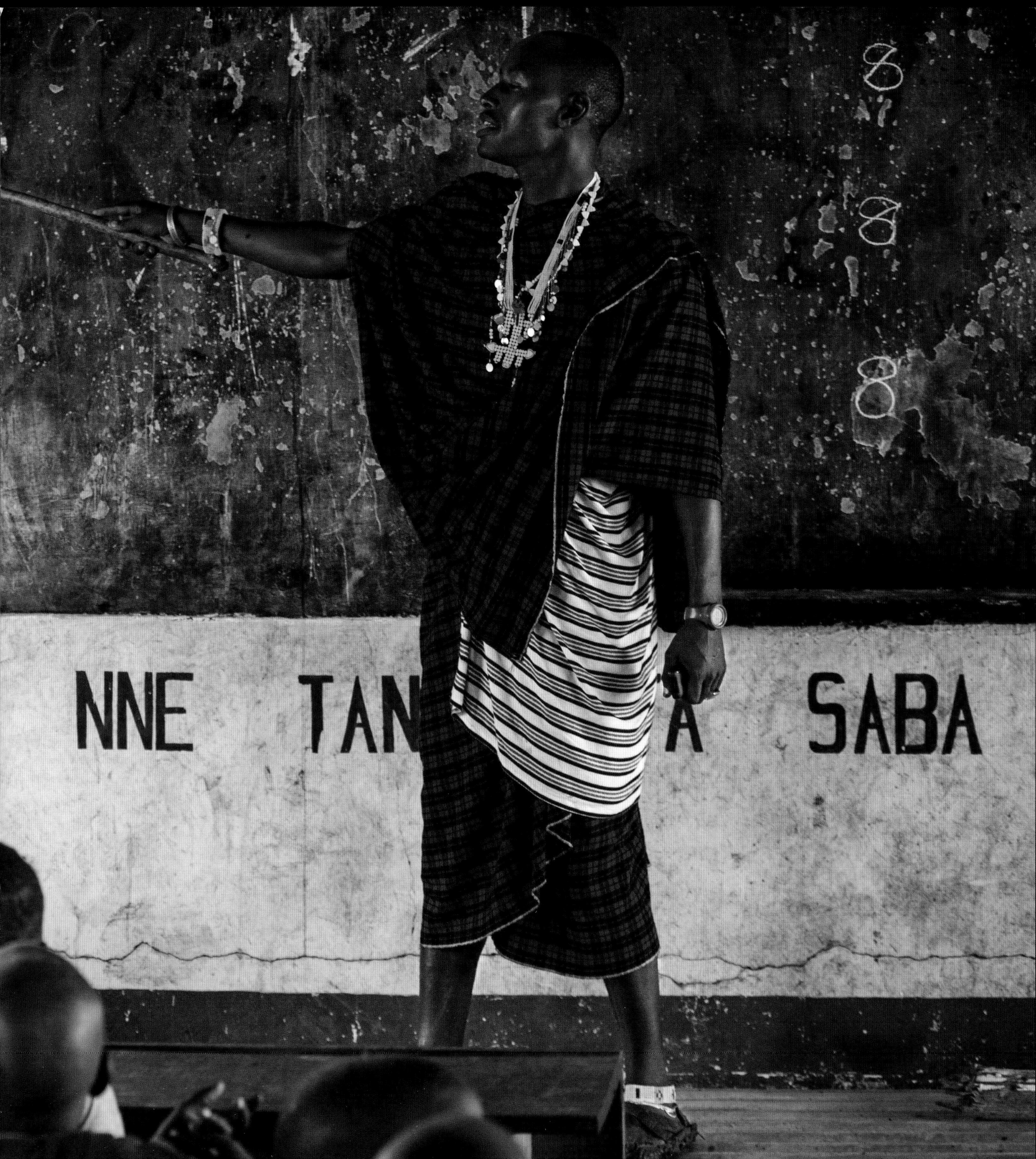
NNE TAN A SABA

**18-19** This school in Orissa (India) is completely without interior furnishings. Each child is equipped only with a cushion which acts as a shelf for the blackboard and a canvas bag that is placed on the ground and which students sit on during the lesson.

**20-21** A Masai teacher patiently guides his class in the foundations of phonetics. The village is quite isolated and many children have to travel a long way to get to school every day.

**22** Intrigued by our unusual presence, the children of Buduwelaka school, on a remote Pacific island, crowd in front of our lenses. Classes are often very numerous and teachers have to manage large groups made up of children of very different ages.

**23** This teacher welcomes us into his long, narrow classroom in a school in Marrakech. The board, used also by the children, is her only precious working instrument.

**24-25** In Myanmar, monasteries have a decisive role in the education of young people. The monks that teach are responsible for about one hundred thousand students across the country, following them with commitment and dedication, and focusing on liberal arts instruction.

**25** Many of the students housed in the ancient Shwe Yan Pyay Monastery (Myanmar) are orphans or come from very poor families who are not able to finance the studies of their children in any other way.

# Booksellers

FOREVER GUARDIANS OF CULTURE, MORE OR LESS
PASSIONATE COLLECTORS OF VARIOUS FORMATS OF PAPER
OBJECTS, BOOKSELLERS CHALLENGE DUST, MOISTURE
AND DISORGANIZATION, CREATING BONA FIDE CULTURAL
REALMS WITH SPECIAL-STATUS. FAR FROM COMPUTER
ARCHIVES AND WAREHOUSE MANAGEMENT WITH AUTOMATIC
REORDERING, THE BOOKSELLERS WE ENCOUNTERED
IN OUR TRAVELS ALMOST CAME ACROSS AS CUSTODIANS
OF KNOWLEDGE. AT TIMES THEY SELL AND ORGANIZE
ITEMS THAT THERE IS APPARENTLY NO DEMAND FOR,
OFTEN ENTRENCHED BEHIND A PRIMORDIAL CHAOS OF PAPER,
WITH LIMITED AND, AT TIMES, ONE-OFF OFFERS.
HOWEVER, IF WE TAKE THE TIME TO DELVE INSIDE THOSE
OPAQUE GLASS CABINETS OR TO GO BEYOND THE PERIMETER
OF A TINY STALL, WE CAN OFTEN DISCOVER AN ENTIRE
WORLD. THERE IS ALMOST ALWAYS SOMEONE READING
A BOOK, ALTHOUGH THEY ARE NOT NECESSARILY BUYERS.
SURPRISINGLY, THE CALM ENERGY OF THE BOOKSELLER
KEEPS THE SITUATION UNDER CONTROL, AWAITING
NEW PASSIONATE READERS.

**26-27** A historical Cuban bookstore overlooks an alley
in the city of Santiago. Inside, you can breathe the history and magic of
the country, while the face of Che Guevara dominates most
of the yellowed covers of the books.

**28** The city of books, also known as Boi Para, can be found near the
university district of Kolkata (India). It is a huge open air market for used
books that stretches along the streets for about a kilometer and a half,
further animating the already bustling College Street.

**29** Boi Para is the largest market for used books in the world. Placed
mostly on shelves, exposed in stands or even stacked on the ground, the
books are sometimes left open in the sunlight to rid them of moisture and
can be re-sold at a modest price to students eager for knowledge.

# Storekeepers

Always standing gossiping in the doorway, bored and busy checking out the passersby and scrutinizing the street, quiet and huddled on tiny stools, working hard to keep up with the bookkeeping. Despite the endless variations in their work, storekeepers throughout the world still embody the essence of commerce. Trading, buying, quantities; seeking to identify shared tastes. A stream of things and money pass through their hands, as do desires that inevitably influence the patterns of human society. It is from their mouths that the price takes shape, often discussed and negotiated. Their behavior generates trust, loyalty, human relationships. The storekeepers we met always allowed us to enter their kingdoms, at times with the hope of a sale, at times just to show us their treasures; always ready to share lots of interesting details. With a few simple gestures, many of them reminded us that goods are just goods, while people are quite another thing

**30-31** To create a store in India, very little is needed: a small cabinet and a tiny table that acts as a shelf, a seat and a counter. To complete the structure, there is an inevitable place to store water, a weak light bulb and a wire on which to hang some of the goods.

**32** This small shop, which is located in the West Bengal region, it is home to different activities. On the ground floor, there is a sort of shop offering refreshments, while the first floor is home to woven baskets that are then sold and used for various purposes.

**32-33** To gain access to the workshop on the upper floor, you must use a ladder, while several wooden poles act as supports for the shutters. These small stores are open long hours and often those who work there also live inside.

**34**  Where space is very limited, some activities also take advantage of tiny bits of wall between two buildings. This man sits and works on a small shelf raised off the ground which in turn supports a small display case with offers of tobacco, sweets and candies.

**35**  This family has turned a room of their house into a kind of store selling vegetables and timber products that have been produced and collected by them.  The women take care of the sales during the day while the men are busy in the fields.

# Recyclers

Perhaps one of the least regulated and safeguarded informal jobs can be found hiding in the nooks and crannies of the metropolis, in the suburbs, in the cramped spaces of large slums. Non-regulated recycling often has a huge social impact and inevitably involves the weakest workers. And in these places, without any regulations, the most disadvantaged people, mostly women and children, separate, select, break down, clean and store huge amounts of materials; waste generated by a consumer society. Materials are reborn thanks to the contribution of these manual workers, generating a disturbing business that is also capable of crossing national boundaries. It's difficult not to feel involved when assisting these transactions. It's impossible not to think about consumption; about its excesses and lack of planning and foresight in the choices made across the world.

**36-37** In countries with developing economies, there is certainly no mention of the recycling industry. The collection and separation of waste is done entirely by hand by thousands of individuals belonging to the poorer classes and very often using female and child labor.

**38-39** In these subterranean tunnels of Mumbai or in sheds without windows, groups of women work more than twelve hours a day to separate various types of plastic. A foreman checks that the pace of work is constant and that there are no errors in the division of materials and colors.

**39** Thousands of "gold panners" search through the city dumps for scrap plastic. This great mass of recyclable fragments is dumped into large hatches along the perimeter of the *slums* and is added to the mountain of waste that rises above the women who select and separate it.

# Undertakers

Death is an inevitable milestone in any culture,
and the rituals and services related to it are faithful
anthropological mirrors. We participated
many times in these socially relevant moments,
always discovering very different patterns.
The element that affected us the most about this
informal world is that often taboos tend to fade,
giving way to more explicit celebrations, at times
even to playful behavior. Often we simply saw
the focus shift towards the tastes and choices
of the deceased, rather than complying with
socially approved procedures. The undertakers
that we happened to watch therefore surprised us,
entertained us, impressed us, and they succeeded
in breaking down many barriers, especially
those of our fears.

**40-41** Not everyone can afford a limousine as part of the final trip for the dearly departed. The coffin can certainly be carried by hand by a small procession of friends, but the cemetery is sometimes very far away and this is not possible. In southern Togo, one company therefore proposes an acceptable and economical intermediate solution.

**42-43** The customized funeral coffins that some agencies of Ghana give their clients are famous throughout Africa and customers often come even from neighboring countries such as Togo and Benin.
As a result of this external influx, funeral agencies of this type have recently multiplied throughout the country.

**43** In Ghana, funeral containers are modeled to the shape chosen by the deceased before moving on to a better life. Often the reference is to the type of work that was done: a stationer will have an enormous ball-point pen, a bartender a bottle of beer, or a mechanic a small car, all of which are nonetheless able to contain their remains.

# With the Hands

chapter 2

There is no doubt that the hands are the principal instrument of work, the primeval mothers of all implements, which they created and then utilized. They are the first evolutionary spark of man who began to produce by making use of the elements surrounding him. Human hands grasp, separate, leave, join, bind, transform, knead and build, and they conduct man through the course of his evolution and occupations. Aristotle called the hands "the instrument of instruments," and precisely due to its potential to become every instrument it holds, he compares it to nothing more or less than the soul itself. At the same time, the great philosopher posed a circular dilemma: is man the most intelligent animal because he has hands, or has he perhaps evolved hands because he is the most intelligent animal? During our worldwide experiences, we have seen extraordinary hands invent creative processes, become skilled, specialized, shape the environment, adapt to various conditions, and model reality. Every movement they made sometimes seemed to be a miracle, a kind of divine proof, the essence of evolved humanity that at times, with the symbolic power of a movement, is able to eliminate everything terrible man is capable of constructing with these very hands. Thus, the master Aristotle proposed a solution to the dilemma: nature has given man hands because he is a being who is able to use them. This statement is like a pertinent lesson that has been passed on to our present age and condition, and we never fail to be amazed and fascinated by the hands that, when necessary, become a sword, horn, claw, spear, pincer and whatever other instrument that has yet to be created.

# Electricians

WORKMEN, ARTISANS OR, MORE SIMPLY, OPERATING
PERSONNEL; THE ELECTRICIANS IMMORTALIZED
BY OUR CAMERAS OFTEN STAND OUT FOR THEIR VERSATILITY.
FAR FROM THE RIGID DIVISIONS BETWEEN THE CIVIL
AND INDUSTRIAL SECTORS, EVERYWHERE WE WENT
WE SAW THEM INSTALLING, REACTIVATING, EVEN CONNECTING
WITH A TOTAL ABSENCE OF MATERIALS, RESOURCES OR
APPARENT LOGIC. GIFTED WITH A GENIAL OVERALL VISION,
THEY ARE OFTEN FORCED BY CIRCUMSTANCES TO DO WORK
THAT IS OUTSIDE THE CONFINES OF THEIR JOB, BECOMING,
WHERE NECESSARY, BRICKLAYERS, CARPENTERS AND
PLUMBERS. LIVES SPENT ACCUMULATING, JOB AFTER JOB,
PRACTICAL AND CONSTRUCTIVE EXPERIENCES THAT
ARE NOT POSSIBLE TO ASSIMILATE WITHOUT LEARNING
FROM MISTAKES AND ENDLESS EXPERIMENTATION.

**46-47**  The followers of Hinduism believe in transmigration and think that the souls of people can be reincarnated countless times in other vessels. This electrician from Varanasi, in his little shop carved out of the alleys (*gali*), is applying this philosophical principle to an old electric motor.

**48**  In the Xiayiang Zhen market, in the Chinese region of Guizhou, an electrician from the area is replacing the coils in the motor of a large washing machine. In rural villages, those who practice this craft are always looked upon with admiration, because those who do this job are able to understand the mysteries of science.

**49**  During the night, two electricians are welding a cable onto the carcass of an old electric motor. They have to work very quickly, because in this small workshop in Arunachal Pradesh in the far north-east of India, as in the whole village, electricity is only available for a few hours a day.

# Blacksmiths

Blacksmiths are perhaps the symbol of *doing* something using manual skill. Alchemists, transformers and manipulators are capable of changing the original state of metals and raw materials with their energy, controlling them with the power of fire. Forgers of objects created from nothing, blacksmiths still retain the aura of magic that history has bestowed on them. Often holed up in dark corners, away from light and concentrated on keeping their own small volcano active, they barely protect their faces, as if setting themselves some kind of daily challenge. Dirty and blackened, yet always focused, they were often the ones who gave us the best smiles, surprised by the attention that their work no longer receives from society. Surviving witnesses of the industrial revolution that mechanized their every single gesture, they still fluctuate lightly in the world of manual labor.

**50-51** This blacksmith is helping a colleague weld the corners of a large metal case. We are in the Haddadine souk, the Medina neighborhood of Marrakech which houses the blacksmiths and all the other metalworkers. The smoke-filled air has a pungent smell, but small works of art come to life spark after spark.

**52** An old blacksmith works a block of red-hot metal in his workshop in the district of Maramures (Romania). By repeatedly beating the hot iron, the man will forge the final object, which in this case will be a horseshoe. This technique also gives greater strength to the ferrous material.

**52-53** The blacksmith's son tries to be helpful and in the meantime learns, by playing, the secrets of this work. When he grows up, he will rely on this heritage of knowledge of one of the oldest professions in the world and decide whether to take it up as a trade or to pursue other ventures.

# Mechanics

THE WORK OF MECHANICS HAS ALSO UNDERGONE
AN INCREDIBLE GENETIC MUTATION OVER TIME.
TODAY THIS ACTIVITY, PERMEATED TO SUCH A POINT
BY ELECTRONICS AND AUTOMATION ENGINEERING THAT
MAN HAS ALMOST BEEN EXCLUDED, CAN SOMETIMES STILL
BE FOUND IN ITS MOST ANCESTRAL FORMS. MALFUNCTIONS
PERCEIVED BY LISTENING TO A NOISE, DIAGNOSIS BASED
ON SMELL, PARTS WEIGHED WITH THE HANDS, ADAPTED,
REASSEMBLED OR EVEN COMPLETELY REMOVED BECAUSE
THEY ARE CONSIDERED REDUNDANT. MECHANICS ARE
OFTEN A SMALL AND PERMANENT CENTER OF GRAVITY
FOR NEIGHBORHOODS. THEIR GREASY WORKSHOPS ARE OPEN
EVEN WHEN THEY SEEM CLOSED, AND ARE VISITED DAILY
BY PEOPLE WHO DO NOT REQUIRE ANY KIND OF SERVICE,
BUT WHO THINK THEY HAVE VALUABLE ADVICE TO OFFER.
AT TIMES THE MECHANICS WE MET THROUGHOUT
THE WORLD SEEMED TRUE GENIUSES OF IMPROVISATION,
CREATIVE-OPERATIVE MEN OF GREAT SKILL; MEN WITH
A THOUSAND SOLUTIONS, AT TIMES NOT WITHOUT
THEIR FAULTS, BUT NONETHELESS TALENTED CREATORS
OF POSSIBILITIES.

54-55 The job of a mechanic is somehow exciting. Knowing how to reach into the mysterious mechanisms and make them work again is considered somewhere between magic and surgery. In old Cuba, with its pre-embargo era vintage American cars, every mechanic is invaluable.

56 A street corner can become a workshop in no time and without any problem at all. A true Indian mechanic does not give up easily, and is able to set up a stove whenever needed in the oil sump of an engine, to remove old consumed gaskets.

56-57 This open-air workshop allows this engineer with lots of experience to perform precision repairs on parts of appliances and mechanical elements that have been worn out by time. He has very few essential tools, two acetylene burners and centuries-old knowledge.

IN THE COUNTRIES WE TRAVELLED THROUGH, THOSE WHO WORK WITH SMALL TIMEPIECES ARE MAINLY SPECIALIZED MECHANICS AND SKILLED REPAIRMEN. IN THEIR DAILY LIVES THEY ARE ACCUSTOMED TO REVIVING INANIMATE OBJECTS, TO FINDING SURGICAL SOLUTIONS WITHOUT ALWAYS KNOWING ALL THE TECHNICAL DETAILS, TO PATIENTLY COMING UP WITH THE MOST UNTHINKABLE ALTERNATIVES. THEY ARE ALWAYS BENT OVER THEIR WORK, WEARING ARTIFICIAL EYES TO FIGURE OUT THE SECRETS OF THE MECHANISMS, GIVING THE SAME THEATRICAL ATTENTION TO THE INNER WORKINGS OF A CHEAP MODERN PIECE AS THEY DO TO PRECIOUS ANTIQUES. IN A WORLD THAT REPAIRS THINGS LESS AND LESS IN ORDER TO BUY MORE AND MORE, WATCHMAKERS ARE STILL THE FRONTIER OF A KIND OF PERSONALIZED SOLUTION, A LAST RESORT, AN EXTREME POSSIBILITY.

**58** The expression of serious professionalism that watchmakers take on when wearing a monocle is the same all over the world. Then they shake their heads and, almost always, say that the situation is serious, but that they will try. Using their skilled fingers, they begin to uncover small hidden mechanical parts.

**60-61** Indian watchmakers, however, do not pretend to solve unsolvable mysteries. They do not call on mysterious forces or spare parts that are now impossible to find. They're used to considering time as a circular element. So they smile and say they can repair it anyway. But that it will take time. The time of watches.

# Weavers

WEAVING USED TO CARRIED OUT IN INDIVIDUAL HOUSEHOLDS OR IN SMALL ARTISAN WORKSHOPS. IN THE CONTEMPORARY WORLD, THIS ACTIVITY HAS COMPLETELY DISAPPEARED FROM OUR HOMES AND NEIGHBORHOODS, BECOMING INDUSTRIALIZED, OUTSOURCED, EXPORTED. PARADOXICALLY, IN THE DEVELOPING COUNTRIES THAT TODAY INDUSTRIALLY PRODUCE TEXTILES FOR THE REST OF THE WORLD, WEAVING STILL SURVIVES IN ITS ORIGINAL FORM. LOOMS PLACED UNDER THE WINDOWS OF RURAL HOUSES, MEN AND WOMEN STILL HARD AT WORK CARDING WOOL, SIMPLE WOODEN MACHINERY THAT HAS BEEN WORKING SINCE ANCIENT TIMES. REPETITIVE MOTIONS, A KIND OF MANTRA PASSED DOWN FROM GENERATION TO GENERATION, PERMITTING FAMILIES TO MEET THEIR OWN NEEDS. AN OCCUPATION OFTEN RESERVED FOR WOMEN, THE LOOM WAS ALSO USED TO CREATE DOWRIES FOR DAUGHTERS IN ORDER TO ASSURE THEM A MORE SOLID FUTURE. THE WEAVERS THAT WE HAVE PORTRAYED IN THE IMAGES BELONG TO A PAST THAT ALMOST EXISTS ONLY IN OUR MEMORIES.

**62-63** In Ghanaian villages, strips of *kente* cloth are produced using these rudimentary traditional looms. Each strip has a precise symbolism based culturally on the drawings and colors of the ancient Ashanti people. Then the strips are put together to make larger fabrics or accessories.

**64-65** Amongst the alleys of magic Kolkata, on the edges of the Kumartuli district, hundreds of dilapidated houses hide mechanized textile workshops in their cellars and attics. Only the noise, a dull and continuous ticking like restless insects, gives away the presence of these family-based industries which are in non-stop production.

**66-67** A thread of light that enters from the dirty glass of a window. A woolen thread that follows the warp of an ancient loom. These are two elements that make up the magic of this image frozen in time. We are among the rice fields of Dazhai in southern China. This woman belongs to the Yao ethnic minority.

# Hairdressers

HAIRDRESSERS ARE EVERYDAY ARTISTS IN THE MULTIFACETED
INFORMAL WORLD; SKILLED MANIPULATORS OF DIFFERENT
TASTES AND IMAGES. THEIR SALONS HAVE ALWAYS BEEN
A CROSSROADS FOR SOCIAL GATHERINGS, POINTS OF
REFERENCE FOR VILLAGES AND NEIGHBORHOODS.
MANY WORK DIRECTLY IN THE STREET, SITTING ON
THE STEPS EQUIPPED WITH A RAZOR AND SCISSORS,
OFTEN WITHOUT EVEN THE COMFORT OF A CHAIR.
OTHERS WORK UNDER PORTICOES OR IN SMALL SHOPS,
GLITTERING MODERN KITSCH WONDERLANDS, OR THEY SET
THEMSELVES UP IN SHACKS, DECORATED WITH DRAWINGS
THAT EXPLICITLY ILLUSTRATE THEIR SERVICES.
YOUNG PEOPLE ONLY GO TO A FEW OF THESE PLACES,
SOME ARE RESERVED FOR WOMEN AND OTHERS ARE
FOR MEN ONLY. IN SHORT, HAIRDRESSERS AROUND THE
WORLD LISTEN, KNOW, PROPAGATE AND OFTEN PROVE
TO BE VALUABLE SOURCES OF INFORMATION
FOR OUR REPORTAGE.

**68-69** The place is professional, the technique seems perfect, and the work will definitely be well done. On the face of the hairdresser, you can see a certain pride. It is justifiable: this salon is located in Arunachal Pradesh in the far north of India in a group of small states called "separatists".

**70** A disturbing image: this young barber who is handling an old razor with ostentatious self-confidence does not seem to have the eyes of an eagle. Fortunately, the mirror is being held by the customer so that he can keep an eye on the path of the blade on his throat.

**71** A row of barbers can be found along the tracks of an abandoned station, a few meters from the famous Flower Market in Kolkata. Our interpreter decides that it is the perfect time to treat himself to a shave and allows us to take some nice pictures.

**72**   Opening a barber shop in the area of Konyak, the famous
headhunters, is surely an interesting choice. The room seems
to be elaborately decorated: a large mirror, lotions, combs,
and towels everything needed to take the best care of a warrior
of this fearsome Myanmar tribe.

**72-73**   This workshop set up and furnished by a hairdresser from Bihar,
one of India's poorest states, can hold its own in comparison with the
best salons in Paris. The hanging mirrors, the large green area, and the
hi-tech but stylish armchairs reflect both good taste and a unique vision.

# Potters

POTTERY MAKING HAS ITS ROOTS IN EARLY CIVILIZATION.
WE HAVE PORTRAYED THOSE WHO BEAR WITNESS
TO THIS ANCIENT PROFESSION, THOSE WHO ARE INCREASINGLY
CAREFUL IN THEIR CHOICE OF THE MOST SUITABLE CLAY;
MOISTENING IT AND KNEADING IT TO MAKE IT SMOOTH
AND PERFECT FOR PRODUCING THEIR HANDICRAFTS.
WE OFTEN OBSERVED THE HYPNOTIC MOVEMENT OF THEIR
WHEELS AND THEIR HANDS, DIRTY WITH THE RAW MATERIAL,
SHAPING OBJECTS READY TO CONTAIN, HOLD, PRESERVE.
THE RECEPTACLES, IN ALL THEIR SHAPES AND FORMS,
ARE THEN LEFT IN THE SUN TO DRY AND SUBSEQUENTLY
BAKED TO BECOME STRONG ENOUGH FOR EVERYDAY USE.
BUT WE FOCUSED PARTICULARLY ON THE HANDS
OF THE POTTERS, IN THE MOMENT THEY CREATED
SOMETHING THAT WAS NOT THERE BEFORE, LIKE MAGICAL
ARTISTS, OUT OF SIMPLE EARTH; SOMETHING THAT
COULD PERHAPS ALSO CONTAIN A WORLD THAT TODAY
IS TOO FULL OF CONTRADICTIONS.

**74-75**   Beautiful Pottery Square, the famous square of Bhaktapur (Nepal) where the potters leave their works to dry creating an almost hallucinatory effect, is surrounded by their antiques stores. You can follow all the stages of production, but also buy the terracotta products.

**76**   The homemade potter's wheel of this potter from Orissa, a village overlooking the Bay of Bengal, is simple and effective. The large flywheel is covered with rags that allow the potter to have a firm grip even with hands that are dirty with clay. The central pivot is lubricated with olive oil and not even a single squeak disturbs the work.

**76-77**   Pottery making is an ancestral art: skilled hands that shape the material and the object that takes shape out of nothing is reminiscent of creation stories. Therefore, observing the various steps of the process is always fascinating and the result is surely of high quality.

# Tailors

THE THING THAT STRUCK US THE MOST ABOUT THE ANCIENT TAILORING PROFESSION WAS THE PLACES WHERE THEY WORK. USUALLY VERY LITTLE SPACE IS RESERVED FOR THIS ACTIVITY, AT TIMES NO MORE THAN A TINY SHELF WITH A SEWING MACHINE OR A NARROW PORTION OF THE TABLE WHERE THE FABRIC IS CUT AND ASSEMBLED. AROUND THEM THERE IS USUALLY AN ENTROPIC EXPLOSION; AN EVERYDAY LIFE THAT APPEARS COMPLETELY OBLIVIOUS TO THE WORK OF THESE MEN AND WOMEN. YET THEIR EXPERIENCED HANDS CONTINUE TO MOVE QUICKLY, ACCOMPANYING THE FABRIC, LAYING OUT FLOWING MATERIALS AND COMBINING THEM WITH IDEAS. THE NIGHT HAPPILY EMBRACES TAILORS, AND WE OFTEN SAW THEM WORKING BY THE FEEBLE LIGHT OF A BULB. IN THE BACKGROUND THE REPETITIVE MANTRA OF AN OBSOLETE SEWING MACHINE, ENCOURAGED BY PATIENT HANDS OR THE RHYTHMIC PRESSING OF A WORN OUT FOOT TREADLE.

**78** Along the dusty roads of Benin, a tailor goes in search of customers, bringing all the tools of his trade along with him. Where there isn't much work, having one customer more or one less can directly affect your meals, so remaining in a store waiting on customers is certainly not worth it.

**80** A microscopic workshop in the alleys of Varanasi meets the needs of two generations of tailors. During the day, the mother designs and cuts tailor-made clothes for the neighborhood clientele using patterns and by resting items on a low wooden platform.

**80-81** At night, the daughter sews the cloth cut out by the mother and gives shape to the clothes that the customers will then try on in the early afternoon, guaranteeing the timeframe needed for the adjustments. The sign on the shop says "Clothes tailor-made in one day."

**82**  An example of "industrial processing" in the so-called informal world: a tailor shop in a small village in Myanmar, specializing in robes worn by monks, with workers skillfully cutting orange-colored fabrics.

**82-83**  A laboratory for packaging cotton tank tops in the heart of Kolkata. Seven people work in this underground area that is only nine square meters and which is illuminated by the greenish tubes of neon lights. Six of them work on the machines and one, stretched out on the ground, packages up and fastens the clothes.

# Goldsmiths

Goldsmiths belong to a category that can still be unquestionably defined as artisan. Perhaps, in comparison to other types of businesses, their profession has not changed that much over time, but it has most definitely seen the introduction of a few new technologies. The connection between the eye, hand and imagination is undoubtedly essential for these artisans. The ability to identify and manage precious materials is fundamental, as are hands which experiment, touch, prepare, and an imagination that is able to visualize the end result. Goldsmiths, photographed in their dark workshops, always have a vision of the finished object before they even start to work. Artisans of all that is precious, producers of symbols of social prestige, creators of pledges and life promises, makers of beauty. In their eyes we saw the glow of satisfaction that distinguishes those who still pursue "excellence" in their work.

**84-85** An Indian goldsmith works in his tiny workshop located in the district dedicated to the workers of the most precious metals. To earn a few extra rupees, he has rented the outer wall of his shop to a political party, who has painted its own symbol on it in bright colors.

**86** This craftsman is melting a silver bar with a small gas torch, resting it on a worn cuttlefish bone that protects the wood of the bench. An apprentice is watching his every move carefully, trying to unravel the secrets of this art.

**87** A young goldsmith is carving some figures onto a commemorative plaque. The most prestigious orders often come from the government who frequently commissions trophies, awards, prizes and medals. A silver plated light bulb protects his eyes and allows him to work longer.

**88-89** In this artisan center, located on the outskirts of Tehran, a group of young goldsmith apprentices work on a large bas-relief. Beating the silver with a number of chisels, they copy one of traditional designs that this workshop usually reproduces for very important customers.

**89** Using an ancient Persian plating technique, this master goldsmith is bringing new life to an old tea kettle. We are in Yadz, an ancient city in the heart of Iran, known throughout the country for its top quality craftsmanship and for being an important center of Zoroastrianism.

# Car
# Thieves

INITIALLY IT IS NOT EASY TO SEE THAT THE PEOPLE
IN FRONT OF OUR EYES, THOSE ON WHOM OUR LENS IS
FOCUSED, ARE NOT ACTUALLY HARD-WORKING MECHANICS;
OR AT LEAST NOT ONLY. CAPABLE OF MAKING CAR THEFT
A TRUE PROFESSION, HAVING EXCELLENT TECHNICAL SKILLS
AND A WEALTH OF MECHANICAL KNOWLEDGE,
THESE WORKERS, VERY MUCH ON THE FRINGE
OF THE SYSTEM, PROFESSIONALLY DISSEMBLE VEHICLES
OF ALL TYPES AND THEN RESELL EACH PART SEPARATELY.
THE VARIOUS MECHANICAL COMPONENTS ARE ALWAYS
DEALT WITH RAPIDLY AND WITH EXTREME ACCURACY,
AND EACH PIECE IS SURGICALLY REMOVED TO BE RE-PLACED
ON THE MARKET AND SOLD INDIVIDUALLY.
THE INFORMAL WORLD PROVIDES THESE LAWLESS
MECHANICS WITH AREAS, SPACES AND WORKSHOPS THAT
DO NOT OFFICIALLY EXIST, BUT OF WHICH EVERYONE
SEEMS TO KNOW THE EXACT LOCATION IN THE MOMENT
THAT BUYING AN ORIGINAL PART BECOMES TOO EXPENSIVE.

**90-91** In the middle of chaotic Mumbai, there is a market dedicated to thieves: the Chor Bazaar. You can find everything along its narrow streets, but you can also lose everything. A car left unattended is totally dismantled and distributed as spare parts in more than fifty different shops in less than ten minutes.

**92-93** One of the *chor,* literally "thieves", who works in Chor Bazaar in Mumbai confesses laughingly that, by adding together the cost of the spare parts, reassembling the same car dismantled just one hour before would cost about thirty-five times the original price of the car. Then he goes away with a carburetor in his hands.

# With Appetite

chapter 3

All the energy humans use up in order to produce, market, distribute and eat food is to be found in this chapter, which consists of a group of images that describes the large number of actions required to satisfy one of man's primary needs. In this category, the work people carry out in order to achieve this aim delineates their historic period and restores social and religious meaning as well as a sense of identity. Thus, the impetus given to food, which is renewed every day, does not consider food merely as something that satisfies a physiological need, but describes a society in detail by separation, distinction and selection. This is why we are so fond of plunging into rural marketplaces, handicrafts districts, the wholesale sector, and retail shops and warehouses. But, above all, we love to mingle with the people who produce, prepare and manage food, before the commercialization process begins. Initially driven by necessity and then by taste, over time man has created collective food provision, has specialized in the preparation and consumption of ingredients that are part and parcel of his territory, and has developed an approach to eating with all the preferences this entails. All the above are elements that act as *spices* in the huge melting pot of intentions, between production and consumption, preparation and the marketing of the most varied types of food. In reality, it is precisely these *spices* that determine the taste of the dishes. And, it is in these flavorful settings, in the most diverse areas of the world, that we have enjoyed so many colors, the most intense textures and combinations, rarities, absences and contrasts. We have always been convinced that one can understand a country much better by sitting in a narrow and crowded space in a small family-run restaurant, ordering what most of the others there have ordered and observing the world from this vantage point.

# Restaurant owners

THE WORLD OF DINING OUT THAT WE SEE DURING OUR
REPORTAGES IS MOSTLY REPRESENTED BY STREET FOOD.
THE IDEA OF A CLASSIC RESTAURANT, WHERE YOU CAN
SIT DOWN AND CHOOSE FROM A VARIETY OF DISHES ON A
MENU, DOES NOT BELONG IN THE EVERYDAY LIFE OF A VAST
MAJORITY OF WORLD CITIZENS, WHO USUALLY HEAD
TO DISTRICTS FILLED WITH SMALL STALLS, BOOTHS
AND FOOD TRUCKS. THESE SIMPLE REFRESHMENT
STRUCTURES NOT ONLY OFFER FOOD AT A GOOD PRICE,
BUT ALSO INTOXICATING SENSORY EXPERIENCES THAT
STIMULATE ALL FIVE HUMAN SENSES, AS WELL AS OUR
SENSE OF TIME, OUR AESTHETIC SENSE AND OUR HUMOR.
THIS EXTEMPORANEOUS WAY OF OFFERING AND SELLING
REFRESHMENTS ALWAYS GIVES US A TRUE SENSE OF THE
LOCAL CULTURE; ITS CONTRADICTIONS, ITS WAYS OF
COMMUNICATING. OFTEN WE COULD PAY FOR OUR FOOD
AT THE END OF THE MEAL, AFTER HAVING TASTED
THE QUALITY. WE FREQUENTLY RECEIVED ADVICE, GIFTS,
THE OPINIONS OF THE ELDERLY AND CHILDREN. SOMETIMES
WE WERE MOCKED FOR OUR INGENUITY. IN SHORT,
MORE CASUAL DINING, ONE THAT COMES TO LIFE IN THE
STREETS OF THE WORLD, AMOUNTS TO A KIND
OF *ELSEWHERE*, WHERE HOSTS MEET GUESTS,
WITHOUT ANY DISTANCE BETWEEN THEM AND
WITHOUT INTERMEDIARIES.

96-97   In Indian cities, there is no dining district. Food, or rather the characteristic smell of *masala*,
is present everywhere, always available at any time of day or night. At the first hint of an appetite,
a restaurant owner is ready to offer you whatever you want to eat.

98   In Asian countries, tea is an institution. But the Indians have adapted this drink to their own taste, adding spices
and milk and thus creating the ubiquitous *masala chai*. Even at night, when every other shop is closed, a wisp of smoke
announces the presence of a *masala chai* seller.

99   Long before sunrise, this little shop opens its doors to the first pilgrims who, crossing the ancient *gali*, are headed to the
sacred Ganga to perform their morning ablutions. A restaurant owner cannot offer very much, but a cup of *chai* or a piece
of fruit can be enough to start the day off well.

100-101 In Asian or South American countries, those who have the task of feeding people and offering restaurant services to passers-by know that the job does not have a schedule and that there are no breaks. At any time, residents, tourists or pilgrims can ask to be fed, given drinks, and refreshed. This young man from Bhaktapur in Nepal knows something about this.

# Bakers

It is not easy to meet bakers because they generally work at night, but in many places in the world bread is baked throughout the day, and the people who work to produce this vital food are the same as those who sell it. We have seen them tired, covered in flour, their clothes smelling of that unmistakable aroma of life, making bread in the various forms and variations that are part of local cultures. The daily comings and goings seen in bakeries is different to that encountered in other stores. They are a melting pot of different social classes, and the buying and selling that takes place inside them is never negotiated or challenged like it is for other product categories, because bread is part of a shared social pattern. A bakery is therefore a sort of neutral ground; a place where the normal rules of commerce are temporarily suspended.

102-103   A large oven in the center of a Moroccan city bakes loaves of bread even late at night. One of the bakers sits down for the first time after working for ten hours straight. In a few minutes, his son will arrive to take over the work and he can finally rest.

104   Being a baker in Uzbekistan is not just a job, it is almost an art. Each baker decorates their own bread molds so differently and characteristically that it is a shame to ruin the beautiful designs when it is time to break the bread and serve them at the table.

105   Walking through the narrow streets of Urgut Market, located about forty kilometers from Samarkand, you can find excellent culinary specialties, typical of the many ethnic groups that meet at the market. Nevertheless, the smell of bread ensures that the bakers take first place amongst all kinds of restaurant owners.

# Pastry Chefs

THANKS TO THE SWEET SMELLING PRODUCTS OF PASTRY
CHEFS, WE HAVE BREATHED IN THE HISTORY OF A COUNTRY.
WITH THEIR CHOICE OF INGREDIENTS AND THEIR SECRET
METHODS OF PUTTING THEM TOGETHER, THESE INVOLUNTARY
ALCHEMISTS TELL A STORY OF MIGRATION FLOWS,
INVASION, CULTURAL TRANSFORMATIONS. PERHAPS
ALL THIS IS UNCONSCIOUSLY REFLECTED IN THE DARK OIL
USED TO FRY THE SWEET DOUGH, IN THE INTENSE SMELL
OF HONEY, OFTEN THE BASE INGREDIENT, IN THE
QUESTIONABLE HYGIENE OF DISPLAY CASES BESIEGED
BY INSECTS. FROM A CULINARY POINT OF VIEW,
PASTRY CHEFS PRODUCE WHAT A CULTURE MOST DESIRES,
BECAUSE IT IS A TREAT. WE WERE OFTEN STRUCK BY THE
OPULENCE OF THE DECORATIONS AND THE ABSURD CONTRAST
OF COLORS THAT GARNISH DANGEROUSLY-HIGH PILES
OF SWEET PASTRIES, OFTEN BOUGHT TO SATISFY
OUR EYES RATHER THAN OUR HUNGER.

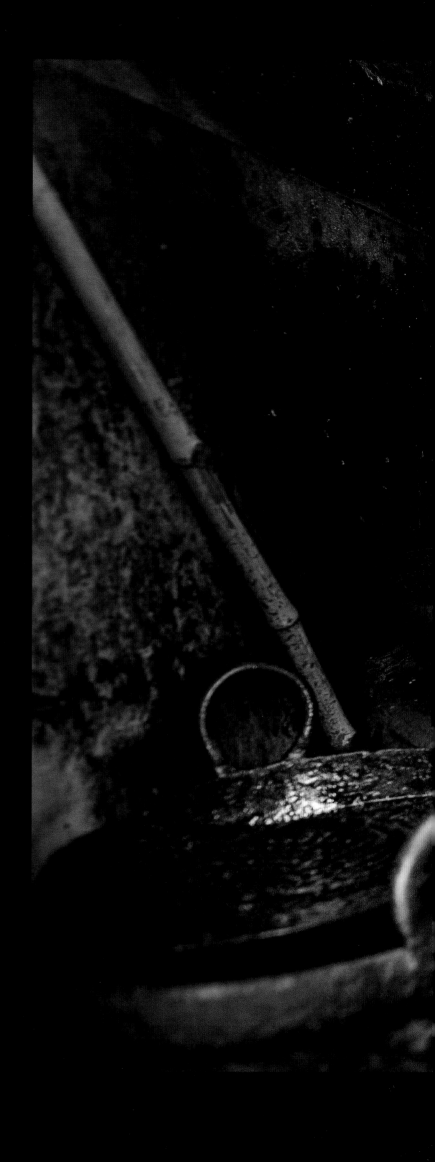

106-107  During our excursions among the *gali*, the tiny streets of ancient Benares, we always stop at the city's historic pastry shop. The sweet pastries in the window, made following the recipes of the owner's father and grandfather, have been the same for four generations.

108  These sweet pastry spirals, fried in oil and honey, require you to take special care before tasting them. But the friendliness of the Indian pastry chef, who in all these years has never failed to offer us a piece, makes us overcome our hesitations each time and even forget about the hygiene-related problems.

108-109  Pastry making in India is an art that seems to be reserved for men only. We never saw a woman or girl at any of the ovens. Even here, the owner's wife is preparing pans that will hold the dough and sesame balls that her husband is carefully frying in the pan.

# Fishmongers

THE FISHMONGERS WE PHOTOGRAPH IN OUR TRAVELS
REPRESENT EVERYDAY INTERFACES. THE GOODS THEY SELL
ARE NOT OF AN EXCEPTIONAL NATURE, BUT OFTEN
THE STAPLE DIET OF THESE POPULATIONS, AND THEREFORE
THE MARKETS WHERE YOU CAN BUY THEM ARE EXTREMELY
POPULAR. THE VARIETY OF FISH BEING SOLD IS LIMITED
BY SEASONALITY AND AVAILABILITY, AND ANYONE WHO
CAN OFFER SOMETHING PRIZED AND DIFFERENT IS ALWAYS
SURROUNDED BY THE VOICES OF A LARGE AUDIENCE OF
BUYERS AND ONLOOKERS. ALL IN A ROW, THESE VENDORS
INVITE POTENTIAL CUSTOMERS TO COMPARE, TOUCH,
OBSERVE AND WEIGH. IN THESE PARTICULAR SITUATIONS,
THE FISHMONGERS HAVE TO BUILD LASTING RELATIONSHIPS
OF TRUST WITH THEIR CUSTOMERS, SO AS TO CREATE GREATER
CUSTOMER LOYALTY, BECAUSE THE TYPE OF GOODS
THEY OFFER, ECONOMIC YET HIGHLY PERISHABLE,
REQUIRES SELLERS AND BUYERS TO MEET FREQUENTLY.

110-111 Korean shops and traditional markets are hidden between the concrete columns of large modern buildings. An ancient world is nestled in these confined spaces. A fishmonger from Gyeondong market, in the center of busy Seoul, occupies the small space between a garage and an elevator.

112 The important fishing port of Manaus supplies a large variety of fish to the general market of the city. Walking among the marble counters taking pictures of the most diverse species of fish can be a pastime that requires hours and definitely promises many surprises.

112-113 The friendliness of the fishmongers at the Manaus market in the Brazilian Amazon is incredible. As good Latin Americans, you only need to give them a look or ask a question and you are immediately regaled with fishing, life, and work stories. In no time at all, they will even share personal stories: wedding pictures mixed in with those of oversized fish specimens.

**114** One of the most fascinating fish markets which we photographed is located in the west of Yemen, in the city of Al Hudaydah. Famous in the past for trading in pearls and coffee, today it is known for this fish market where you can buy an amazing variety of fish.

**115** The best shark fisherman from all over the region come to the Al Hudayah fish market and this justifies both the presence of many customers and that of the many onlookers who come just to see the huge animals. Meanwhile, teenagers unload a variety of fish from huge containers.

# Poulterers

THEY HANDLE LARGE BASKETS CROWDED WITH YELLOW
LEGS AND STARTLED RED CRESTS. THEY PLUCK,
CUT, SEPARATE, WASH, TRIM. THE POULTERERS WE MET
IN OUR TRAVELS ARE NOT JUST SELLERS; THEY TAKE
CARE OF THE ANIMALS FROM BIRTH AND OVERSEE ALL
THE STAGES RIGHT UP TO THE SALE OF THEIR MEAT.
THEY USE RUDIMENTARY TOOLS WITH SURGICAL SKILL,
SO MUCH SO, THAT THEIR EFFECTIVE MOVEMENTS APPEAR
SIMPLE AND LIGHT-HANDED. UNDOUBTEDLY THESE TYPES
OF BUTCHERS WORK WITH THE MOST DIVERSE PUBLIC
IN THE GREAT MOSAIC OF DIFFERENT CULTURES AND
RELIGIONS. CHICKEN IS THE MOST ACCEPTED, SHARED
MEAT IN THE WORLD, FREE FROM THE TABOOS OF BELIEFS
AND RELIGIONS. THE COUNTER OF A POULTERER IS IN EVERY
RESPECT REPRESENTATIVE OF AN ENTIRE COUNTRY,
AND WE OFTEN THINK THAT, IN A CERTAIN WAY,
THE ARTISAN TECHNIQUES STILL USED TODAY KEEP
THE OVERPOWERING LOGIC OF INDUSTRIALIZATION AT BAY.
BUT MAYBE IT'S JUST A MATTER OF TIME.

116-117   In the Tao Jiang market, in China's southwestern region of Guizhou, chicken-sellers have a space just for them. The large baskets not only host chickens of all kinds, but also the vendors themselves, who find it convenient to choose the right chicken to offer from within the basket.

118-119   The Sichuan is a region of central China, bordering the autonomous region of Tibet, that is populated by no less than 53 ethnic groups. The Dawo market is host to many of these populations and it is easy to take part in special culinary traditions such as the charring of chickens by blowtorch.

119   Many clients also buy live chickens, either for breeding or for the production of eggs, but most poulterers provide families with meat for food. Unfortunately for this animal, the chicken is not sacred to any religion nor taboo for any population.

**120** At the New Market in the city of Kolkata, there is a huge industry dedicated to poulterers. Many of them are Muslims, even though chicken is consumed without any problem by both Muslims and Hindus.

**120-121** In Indian markets, poulterers collect chickens in large baskets which can be easily transported with a cart or a bicycle. These containers can be just as easily displayed on the shelves of a market stand or they can be hung up, thanks to the netting that holds the animals in.

# With the Arms

chapter 4

Work inevitably leads to a transformation and re-creation of reality on the part of human beings, and, in this sense, manual labor may perhaps lay claim to superiority over all the other types of occupation. With his arms, man takes on the responsibility of his actions and totally exposes himself. With his arms, he tests the effectiveness of his ideas, the accuracy of his project; he sees the physical result of what he has previously imagined. Manual work is perhaps the kind with the most direct relationship to the materials used, the one that requires more competence and experience. We tried so many times to identify ourselves with the manual work we observed, which was by no means easy. Only through fatigue, repetition, specialization, and closeness to the individual activities can one really understand its essence, almost as if it were a mantra, a spiritual exercise whose sense lies not in the finished product but in the process itself. The expert movements of fishermen, the strength of washerwomen, the physical knowhow of those who, literally, embrace the product of their labor, attracted our attention with their hypnotic power. All of these images ended up in our archives, which were separated into folders that exist only virtually, despite the physical nature of the subjects. On the other hand, we have seen men and women distinguish themselves by touching the materials of their trade, mastering them and, literally, transforming them with the strength of their arms; we have seen them excel simply because of the light of the consciousness of their work that shines in their eyes. Of course we don't know if this is the same light we have captured with our cameras, but we certainly did not let it elude us. Maria Montessori once stated that manual labor with a useful purpose could help one acquire interior discipline. Some of our photographs seem to confirm this.

# Fishermen

THE POPULAR CULTURE OF FISHERMEN IS BASED ON THE FACT THAT THIS WORK IS CARRIED OUT IN A PARTICULAR ENVIRONMENT, A MARINE ENVIRONMENT, RESULTING IN A WAY OF LIFE AND RULES THAT ARE VERY DIFFERENT TO THOSE OF TRADES CARRIED OUT ON LAND. FISHERMEN ARE OFTEN IDENTIFIED AS ALMOST BELONGING TO A PARTICULAR CASTE, SHARING SECRETS, TABOOS, INFORMATION AND VERY SPECIFIC SKILLS. HAVING VERY LITTLE TECHNICAL SUPPORT IN TERMS OF ASSISTANCE AND TRANSPORT, FISHERMEN IN DEVELOPING COUNTRIES CAN BE SEEN AS SURVIVORS OF COASTAL URBANIZATION AND TOURISTICIZED BEACHES. OUR IMAGES HAVE ALWAYS PORTRAYED THEM IN THE DARKNESS BEFORE DAWN, READY TO FACE ENDLESS DAYS FILLED WITH RISKS, AND IN THE DARKNESS AFTER SUNSET, OFTEN UNLOADING JUST A FEW CRATES OF FISH: THE SOURCE OF THEIR MEAGER EARNINGS.

**124** The fishermen from Lake Inle, located in the mountains of Shan State in Myanmar, seem to dance on the extreme edges of their boats. The cone-shaped lobster pots, traditionally used for fishing, help create the idea of weightlessness, as if the fishermen were clinging to them and not vice-versa.

**126-127** Lake Inle is inhabited by the Intha people, the sons of the lake, that cut across its surface by rowing their boats in a very particular way: they remain standing up on the bows using a single oar, helping to push the boat along with one leg and as a result of these movements, they end up looking like marsh birds at sunset.

**128-129** The settlements of fishermen on the beaches of Biriwa, in the south of Ghana, stand out for the blue-green color of their super-fine fishing nets. Inevitably, teenagers play on these soft surfaces and adults give in to a well-earned rest.

**129** In front of every house, large skeins that seem to be clouds on earth can be seen hung out to dry on the boats that have just come in from the sea. The sea here is generous and no family goes hungry, but it is a labor-intensive work and the fishermen have to start each day even before the dawn breaks on their nets.

**130-131** The fishermen of the Gopalpur village in the Indian state of Orissa have a serious problem to deal with every morning. On one hand, the fish-rich sea of the Bay of Bengal gives them enough to live on, but on the other hand, it seems to be very jealous of its treasures.

**131** The gulf current here produces a special wave which is very high and dangerous, making it very difficult for fishing boats to launch during the hours when they would normally start fishing. Only a few boats every morning manage to overcome the wave. For the others, it is a day of fasting.

**132-133** Chinese fisherman from Yangshuo, in the northeast of Guangxi, are now famous all over the world for their habit of entrusting the challenging part of their work to obliging trained cormorants. The birds, skilled fishers, identify the fish and catch it by diving to then bring it to the crafty trainer.

**133** To prevent the cormorants from swallowing the fish they catch, a metal ring is placed around their neck tight enough so that the catch, too big to go down their throat, remains in their beak and ends up in the basket of their owner. The birds are then rewarded with a fish small enough to pass the obstruction.

# Washer-persons

WASHER-PERSONS STILL EXIST, HIDDEN AMONG
THE FOLDS OF THE SYSTEM, IN A LARGE PART OF THE WORLD
THAT HAS NOT YET DELEGATED THIS JOB TO INDUSTRIAL
MACHINES, OR AT LEAST NOT ENTIRELY. OUR PHOTOGRAPHS
SHOW THESE FOREVER BUSY WORKERS COLONIZING
UNSUSPECTED PLACES AND MANAGING UNBELIEVABLE
AMOUNTS OF CLOTHES. WHAT IS SURPRISING IS THAT EVEN
THE INSTITUTIONALIZED WORLD OF WORK, LIKE COMPANIES,
LARGE HOTELS OR LARGE INDUSTRIAL LAUNDRIES,
USE THESE INCREDIBLE UNSTRUCTURED LAUNDRIES,
AT TIMES HOUSED IN BASEMENTS, AT TIMES SET UP OUTSIDE,
WHERE GROUPS OF WEARY WORKERS RUB AND SCRUB THE
CLOTHES BY HAND, BEATING THEM VIGOROUSLY
AND RHYTHMICALLY AGAINST LARGE SMOOTH STONES.
USUALLY RESERVED FOR MEN, THE TRADITIONAL WORK
OF A WASHER-PERSON IS ABLE TO SURVIVE ANYTHING,
EVEN THE MOST MODERN TECHNOLOGIES.

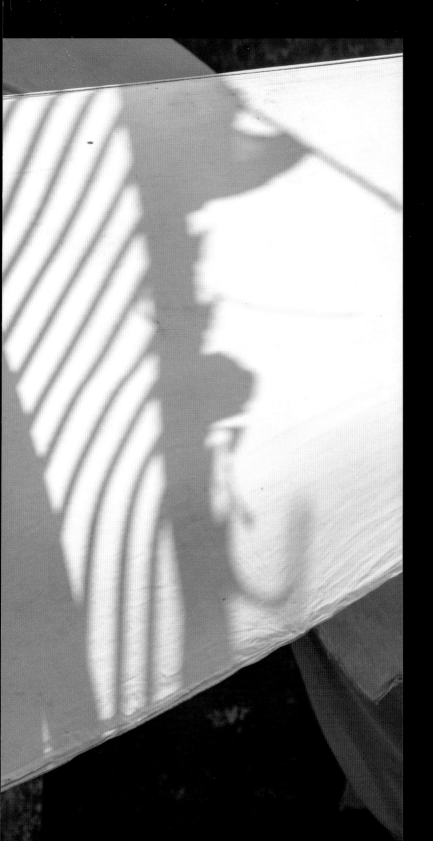

**134-135** Approximately 10,000 people, called *dhobi*, work in this
washing-city called *Dhobi Ghat*, in the heart of Mumbai.
Over top of a thousand blocks made into concrete tubs, the tireless
arms of generations of washer-people have rinsed, beat and squeezed
out the laundry of an entire metropolis.

**136-137** Indian cities that do not have laundromats organized as they
are in Mumbai at least have a flow of water where people can launder
their own sheets and saris. To dry these fabrics quickly, the women hang

**138**  For anyone involved in washing clothes, access to water is a fundamentally important factor. These washer-people from the village of Tiebele, Burkina Faso, are forced to walk for almost two kilometers with their loads on their heads and children on their backs to reach the closest usable well.

**138-139**  A group of women from Gujarat have washed their families' clothes in the water of an artesian well. To dry these clothes in the wind and sun, some shrubs are provided that keep the clothes off the ground and out of the sand so as not to negate the work done.

# Gold
# Panners

MEN IMMERSED IN THE WATERS OF SACRED RIVERS SIFTING
THE ASHES OF DEAD BODIES, DAY AND NIGHT,
IS AN ESTABLISHED TRADITION IN INDIA.
ONCE THE FUNERAL PYRE IS EXTINGUISHED,
THESE UBIQUITOUS WORKERS, WHO BELONG TO
THE LOWEST SOCIAL CLASS, ARE AUTHORIZED TO PROCESS
THE ASHES OF THE DEAD WITH THE HELP OF A RUDIMENTARY
SIEVE. THEY SEARCH FOR WHOLE BONE FRAGMENTS
TO GIVE TO THE RELATIVES FOR FURTHER RITUALS
AND PRAYERS, MAYBE EVEN FINDING PIECES OF JEWELRY
OR TEETH WITH GOLD CROWNS, WHICH THEY ARE ALLOWED
TO KEEP AS COMPENSATION FOR THEIR WORK.
A SPECIFIC PLACE IN SOCIETY IS RESERVED FOR THESE
WORKERS, INTIMATELY CONNECTED TO FUNERARY RITES,
WHICH CLEARLY REVEALS THE ONGOING SHADOW
OF THE ANCIENT CASTE SYSTEM. INDEED, ONLY THE *DALITS*,
THE UNTOUCHABLES, ARE ALLOWED TO HANDLE
THE CORPSES DURING FUNERAL RITES. BOTH AN HONOR
AND A CONDEMNATION.

140-141   In India, the sacred task of cremating bodies
is entrusted to the castes of untouchables, such as
*dom*. After they have burned the body, they recover the
ashes and dry them out carefully. If they find gold teeth
or some other valuable jewel, the untouchables are
authorized to keep them.

# Dyers

WITH THEIR BARE HANDS INSIDE THE VATS, IMMERSED IN COLOR, THEY LIFT THE HIDES FROM BOILING HOT POTS, DRY THEM,
MIX COLORS THAT AT TIMES ARE TOXIC, HANG WOOLS AND FABRICS WITH A KALEIDOSCOPE OF COLORS.
IN MANY COUNTRIES DYERS RISK THEIR LIVES, DAILY WORKING IN CONTACT WITH CHEMICALS THAT ARE NOT PERMITTED ELSEWHERE,
CORROSIVE EFFLUENT, BUCKETS THAT GIVE OFF FUMES, GASES, VAPORS. YET IN MANY SOCIETIES WHERE THIS PROFESSION
IS STILL CARRIED OUT ARTISANALLY, DYERS ALSO COLOR LEATHER AND FABRICS BY HAND FOR THE REST OF THE WORLD.

# With Sweat

chapter 5

In our technological age, physical fatigue has almost become extraneous to work, since it is now the prerogative of an ever-decreasing minority of workers. And even here this type of exertion has, over time, been mitigated and regulated, made more and more bearable, to the point of almost being its sublimation. It is as if contemporary humankind, which is becoming increasingly more technological and fluid, were gradually liberating itself from hard work and pain, and, perhaps unconsciously, seeking to distance itself from death as well. The fact is that we First World workers earn our living in better and better conditions, comforted by all kinds of facilitation. Although it is undeniable that the quality of life has improved, we pay a price for this, allowing our sensory capabilities to fade away little by little. We can see our practical skills gradually decrease day by day – skills and competences that entire generations used to build a historic patrimony of progress. In order to limit exertion, we let others to tell us how to work allowing them to impose the timetable and the very purpose of our work. The lives of our ancestors are mirrored in the sweat produced by hard work, which is part and parcel of our history, our origins, the DNA of our activity. Now, the work whereby grandchildren earn a living does not seem in the least related to the work carried out by their grandfathers. Technology has also altered the very essence of work forever, and we have now become almost used to paying in order to work up a sweat, making it a leisure time activity. This brings to mind the disturbing discourse of Richard Marc Emerson, who theorized the end of the human race due to too much civilization.

# Brick makers

These workers' days are endless. Before dawn, the men, although actually mainly women and children, start to work on shaping, molding, cooking, drying and transporting the heavy blocks of clay. Dozens of families live in symbiosis with the furnace, camping inside the extensive enclosing walls so as to manage the intense work sessions in the best possible way. The furnace operators start work at a very young age and build up their experience day by day, learning to correctly handle the raw material. Looking at these hundreds of sweat-beaded foreheads, we are amazed at the thought that many of the bricks used to build large buildings in the downtown areas of these countries, are still manufactured manually and, above all, artisanally.

**151** Whole families work, live, and are born in the vast brick factories that dot the outskirts of Kolkata. The production cycle has no breaks and every day, for 24 hours straight, the hands of women, children, adult men and the elderly knead, load, select, move, and bake bricks.

**152** In this type of community, perhaps it does not make sense to speak about child labor. Women carry newborns around without ever stopping working, but the conditions are not inhumane. The families live together and the younger ones learn to work while simultaneously playing and learn to play while working.

**152-153** For each cargo that is transported, there is a plastic disk. For each group of bricks put into the furnace, there is another diskette. Even each basket of crushed rock thrown out of the factory has a disk. In the evening, a foreman whistles to signal the end of the shift and converts the disks in rupees. The more disks there are, the more rupees are given out, and hunger is kept far off.

# Fertilizer Producers

IT IS WELL-KNOWN THAT SCRAP LEATHER IS AN EFFECTIVE FERTILIZER MATERIAL. IN DEVELOPING REGIONS, WORKERS WORK WITH UNDENIABLE RISKS TO THEIR HEALTH. RECYCLING PROCEDURES AND TREATMENTS ARE NOT PROVIDED FOR BY SMALL PRODUCTION COMPANIES. WASTE MATERIALS, TURNED INTO ASHES, ARE TRANSPORTED, HANDLED AND BAGGED MANUALLY BY MEN WHO OFTEN SPEND MOST OF THEIR LIVES DOING THESE JOBS. UNDOUBTEDLY THE QUALITY OF LIFE FOR MEN WORKING IN THE INFORMAL WORLD IS REDUCED TO THE BARE MINIMUM, AND IT IS UNLIKELY TO IMPROVE IN AN INDUSTRY THAT RARELY INNOVATES OR INVESTS, BUT INSTEAD DAILY EXPLOITS EXPERIENCES AND TRADITIONS.

**155** The processing of leather waste into fertilizer is a common practice throughout the world. The cutouts tanned with chromium are collected into large deposits and burned in furnaces that turn them into an extremely effective ash with uncommon agronomic characteristics.

**156-157** The effects of the use of chromium on human health are the subject of lengthy discussions and generate large disparities in attitudes in international law. Moreover, in the rest of the world, this process is normally carried out by machinery and by personnel in safe working conditions.

**157** Men who live on the outskirts of Indian cities, in this case a few kilometers from Kolkata, breathe in the fumes caused by the tanning of leather for 12 hours per day and have no other protective measures than a handkerchief wrapped around their head. In contrast, they have the certainty of a job that many people would not do.

# Porters

PERHAPS THE SYMBOL OF FATIGUE, OF MANUAL PRODUCTION, OF THE TRANSFORMATION OF BODY ENERGY
TO PERFORM A JOB. PORTERS ARE WIDELY REPRESENTED IN THE WORLD OF NON-REGULATED ACTIVITIES.
UNBELIEVABLE LOADS, AT TIMES MANAGED WITH INCREDIBLE DEXTERITY, OFTEN RELYING ON HUGE EXERTION.
THRONGING MARKETS, CROWDING OUTSIDE FACTORIES, IMPENETRATING THE WORLD OF AGRICULTURE;
PORTERS OFFER SUPPORT ACROSS VARIOUS DIFFERENT SECTORS. THEORETICALLY YOUNG AND STRONG,
BUT IN REALITY OLDER AND PHYSICALLY TESTED BY A LIFE OF TOIL, THEY ARE LIVING PROOF
OF JUST HOW MUCH MANUAL LABOR IS AND ALWAYS HAS BEEN A MAINSTAY OF THE WORLD.

**159** Leaving aside common stereotypes, Indian porters are slender, lightweight, and almost fragile. It almost seems as if an external force supports the enormous loads that they are able to carry on their bony backs.

**160** Many times we observed porters who endlessly, using only the strength of their backs and their legs, moved tons of goods, vegetables, and fruit from containers in trucks to market warehouses. Silently, one after the other, with never a complaint, each of them found the strength to smile before the camera.

**160-161** There are few tools that help the porters of developing countries: a towel over their shoulders to increase friction and prevent the load from sliding to the sides, a rolled up towel on their head to distribute the weight over their whole skull, and the inevitable hook with which they firmly grasp bags and baskets.

**162**   The porters of the fishing port of Manaus, on the banks where the Rio Negro meets the Amazon River, are true acrobats. Helped by special boxes for fish fitted with joints, they can carry up to five containers on each single trip.

**162-163**   Heavy crates of fish are all numbered to identify the vessel of origin. Each porter has special headgear on his head that helps to distribute the weight of the load evenly to the neck and shoulders without weakening the back.

# With the Legs

chapter 6

Humans are erect, walk, and choose where to go and move about with their legs; but by so doing they become somewhat nomadic, seeking something in their primordial genetic makeup. Working with one's legs not only means using them physically, but also changing your position in space, following a kind of necessary cosmic movement, taking a path, living by moving things and persons. Nowadays, we use our legs less and less in our various activities, yet many human occupations represent their essence. Despite the many times we have observed, photographed and lived close to people who run every day – pulling a rickshaw or cart with passengers or merchandise, men pedaling and asking for directions, or walking briskly, pushing their way with their legs, avoiding obstacles and moving forward with an ancient and infinite movement – we never fail to be surprised. In a certain sense, these people seem to suggest a different awareness and knowledge of our common act of getting about and moving. Yet, legs seem to be the only plausible means to carry out certain occupations that are quite common in the informal economy. It is impossible to get about in some Asian cities without these 'men-horses'; one cannot make do in the total chaos of public transport in India without those ticket vendors who climb up onto the seats on the run and tear off your ticket while still running; again, one simply must move one's stall and merchandise around in crowded places where the people themselves are moving around frenetically and where there is no available space or, even should such space exist, there is no way of getting there. In short, as our former existence as *Homo erectus* has taught us, work still depends upon our legs: they lay claim to man's right to exist in space, without mediation and without implements. Basic and effective, a cornerstone of the evolution of our species, legs still represent, for a large number of men and women the world over, the principal, indispensable instrument of their occupation.

# Hawkers

THE NOMADIC GENETIC MAKEUP OF THESE WORKERS
IS STILL SKIN-DEEP. ENDLESSLY ON THE MOVE,
HAWKERS ARE SELF-SUFFICIENT CELLS THAT CONTINUOUSLY
ADAPT TO ANY REALITY. SHREWD AND BRILLIANT,
ABLE TO FIND UNPRECEDENTED OPERATIONAL SOLUTIONS,
HAWKERS ALWAYS HAVE A DEEP KNOWLEDGE
OF THE TERRITORY. THEY CAREFULLY STUDY PEAK TIMES,
PEDESTRIAN FLOW, ADAPTING, UNDERSTANDING
AND SHAPING LOCAL TASTES. WHETHER THEY SELL FOOD,
CLOTHING OR OFFER SERVICES; WHETHER THEY MANAGE
A TABLE, A CART, OR JUST A BASKET; THEY HAVE
ALWAYS HAD A VERY DIRECT RELATIONSHIP WITH PEOPLE,
THEREBY HAVING A WEALTH OF DEEP EMOTIONAL
UNDERSTANDING.

**166-167**  Among the endless rows of stands, among the
thousands of products lying on the ground and among the
many tables upon which lie all kinds of goods, in the largest
market in Kumasi, Ghana's second largest city, a man
selling remote controls  passes with his kaleidoscope
of technology suitable for any circumstance.

**168**  This young man from Mopti, a sweltering city
in the center of Mali, has invented an interesting job.
He has created a mobile pharmacy able to reach customers
easily. At the exit of the airport, in fact, the young
entrepreneur offers his products to tourists,
with astringent medicines at the forefront.

**168-169**  In Bobo Diulasso, a town in southern Burkina
Faso, it is not easy to sell your own wares. Becoming
mobile is almost a necessity, because your store can then
be magically packed into a suitcase from which, at the right
moment, you can take out supports and umbrellas, and
then move it to wherever there are people.

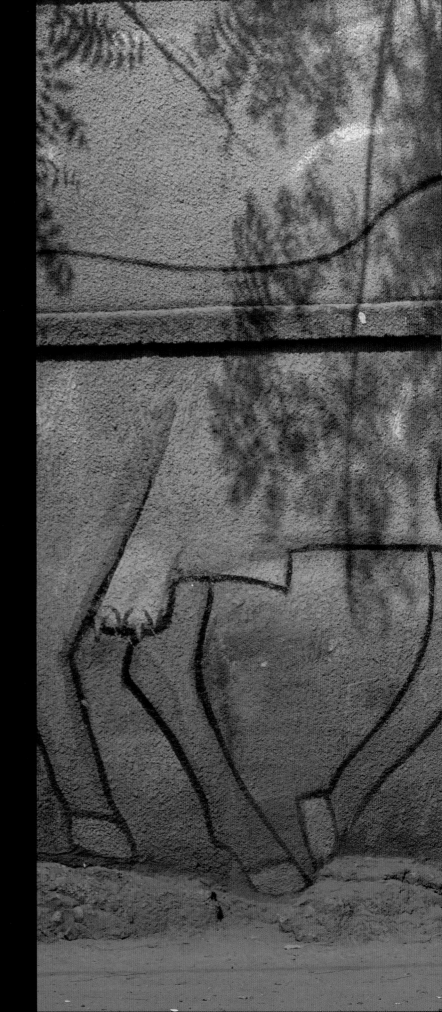

170   The knife grinder goes wherever there is need, especially
to the many food markets that dot ancient Kolkata, where blades are
used until they are worn out and the purchase of a new knife is a serious
affair, to be decided calmly and in agreement with business partners
and family members.

171   The *rikshaw-bike* is often used exclusively to load goods to be
transported. The owners hardly ever get up on it to start pedaling,
but walk at its side to be more agile in traffic and to make it more
efficient, and if necessary, to brake.

172   This simple system of making a wooden table movable is common
in the whole of North India and allows for the use of simple bicycle
wheels. The real engine is the owner's legs which, when they have
finished their journey, can be rested on the vehicle.

172-173   The Sonepur Fair, in southern Bihar (India), is held at
a very hot muggy time of year. Visitors can hardly resist buying a cold
drink, especially when an enterprising street vendor follows them
under the relentless sun.

# Fruit and Vegetable Vendors

FRUIT AND VEGETABLE VENDORS IN RURAL MARKETS,
AS WELL AS IN THOSE IN CHAOTIC METROPOLITAN AREAS,
LIVE IMMERSED IN THE COLOR OF THEIR PRODUCTS.
THEY BUILD PILES OF FRUIT AND VEG THAT DEFY GRAVITY;
THEY ORGANIZE, STACK, PICK UP, CLEAN AND POLISH THEIR
PRODUCE. WATER IS THEIR ELEMENT *PAR EXCELLENCE*,
WITH WHICH THEY PRESERVE THEIR GOODS, STORE THEM,
IMPROVE THEM AND MAKE THEM MORE ATTRACTIVE.
THEY USE WATER TO ENHANCE THE COLORS, TO MAKE
THE SURFACES SHINE, TO CELEBRATE THE SEASONS.
OFTEN ALSO FARMERS AND PRODUCERS, FRUIT AND
VEGETABLE VENDORS ARE INVOLVED IN ALL THE STAGES
OF THE LIFE CYCLE OF THE PRODUCTS THEY SELL, AND THEY
ALWAYS LOOK AT THEIR STALLS WITH A CERTAIN PRIDE.

174-175   In hot countries, fruits and vegetables tend to wilt quickly. The leaves wither, the surfaces become dark, the pulp is oxidized and the products are no longer appealing. It is therefore necessary to moisten them often to give them new life. The problem is always finding an adequate supply of water.

176   The lake dwelling village of Ganvie, in the south of Benin, has about 30,000 inhabitants, who need to buy goods and offer business in various shops. Lacking the mainland, the floating markets are the only plausible solution, simple and easy to use by any village member.

177   This farmer from Sundarbans in Bangladesh is proud of his products. His work is not easy because the ground where he lives and works is an infested mangrove swamp. The production of zucchini of this size is therefore an exceptional outcome that can be seen in his expression.

**178**  Mumbai boasts an exceptional fruit and vegetable market, famous throughout the city and open 24 hours a day. Thousands of people work in this maze of concentric courts where the farmers bring, display and sell their own products at an incredible rate.

**178-179**  In Mumbai, there is also a general market called Crawford Market. Here the goods are exposed more neatly and buyers have time to stroll and observe quietly. Food products are placed on benches with great care, sorted and polished under the multicolored lights of plastic sheeting.

# Rickshaw Pullers

IT IS HARD TO IMAGINE CERTAIN CITIES, ESPECIALLY IN ASIA, WITHOUT RICKSHAW PULLERS.
THEY WHIZZ AND DODGE THROUGH CRAZY TRAFFIC, ALLOWING PEOPLE TO TRAVEL IN A DIMENSION THAT NO
OTHER MEANS OF TRANSPORT CAN OFFER. CYCLING, SPEEDING, STRUGGLING, OFTEN THESE TRANSPORT OPERATORS
ARE THE ONLY FAST, ECONOMIC AND SUSTAINABLE SOLUTION TO DAILY TRANSFERRING MILLIONS OF PEOPLE IN THE WORLD.
GETTING INTO A RICKSHAW IS ALWAYS AN EXCITING EXPERIENCE, ALLOWING YOU TO SEE CITIES FROM A COMPLETELY DIFFERENT
POINT OF VIEW. THESE SURVIVING TRADITIONAL PROFESSIONS ARE ALMOST ALWAYS PASSED DOWN FROM FATHER TO SON,
RESERVED FOR DISADVANTAGED SOCIAL CLASSES, AND THEREFORE REPRESENTING A FUNDAMENTAL SOURCE
OF INCOME FOR ENTIRE FAMILIES.

180   This form of human-powered transportation in some countries is now considered illegal, but the association of drivers of Kolkata, where there is the largest rickshaw fleet in the world, strongly opposed this prohibition. To follow the rules, *rikshaw-bikes* and *motor-rikshaws* have been created everywhere.

182   Rickshaws, widespread in Asia and Africa, are a human-powered means of transport whose name derives from the English word *rickshaw*, an adaptation of the Japanese word *jinrikisha* (composed of *jin* = man, *riki* = strength and *sha* = vehicle), which literally means "human-powered vehicle".

182-183   In Japan, the *shafu*, the men pulling the rickshaws, have become true tourist guides. They have to know the history of the country and the monuments they encounter along the way, after which they always issue a certificate showing the calories they have consumed and the savings in terms of pollution.

183

# Truck Drivers

THE WORLD OF TRANSPORT HOLDS A KEY POSITION
IN ALL ECONOMIES. IN THE INFORMAL SECTOR THERE
IS ALSO A MUCH LESS CLEAR-CUT DIVISION BETWEEN PUBLIC
AND PRIVATE TRANSPORT. FLEXIBILITY AND IMPROVISATION
ARE PERHAPS THE MOST REPRESENTATIVE CHARACTERISTICS
OF TRUCK DRIVERS IN THIS PIECE OF THE WORLD.
PASSENGERS ARE TRANSPORTED WITH GOODS, GOODS
ARE TRANSPORTED WITH PASSENGERS, AND AT TIMES GOODS
ARE EVEN ACCOMPANIED BY ANIMALS. OFTEN THOSE
WHO WORK IN TRANSPORTING LIVE AND SLEEP ON
THEIR TRUCK, ABOUT WHICH THEY CARE A GREAT DEAL,
DEDICATING TIME AND ATTENTION TO TURNING IT INTO A
TEMPORARY HOME. ALWAYS FINDING A WAY TO EXCEED
WEIGHT LIMITS, TRUCK DRIVERS ARE ALMOST ALWAYS
SKILLED MECHANICS, ABLE TO CREATE ANYTHING
FROM SPARE PARTS AND MAINTAIN A KIND OF SYMBIOTIC
RELATIONSHIP THEIR VEHICLE.

184-185 Anyone who possesses a means of transport in India is considered a truck driver and offers to carry any kind of goods. The weight, volume or size of the product have no importance. The vehicle will be described as the most suitable and consistent for the purpose regardless.

186 Along the roads of Africa, any means that has a motor is in some way considered common property. The subtle difference between interior spaces and external vanishes at the start, or at least on the way. Things, animals and people are added along the way up to the point of making the vehicle itself invisible.

186-187 The departure of a truck on the dusty roads of Banfora, Burkina Faso, forces the truck driver and passengers to play a difficult game of making space. Those who will stay on the ground also play as they feel compelled to give tips on loading and on the trip to be taken.

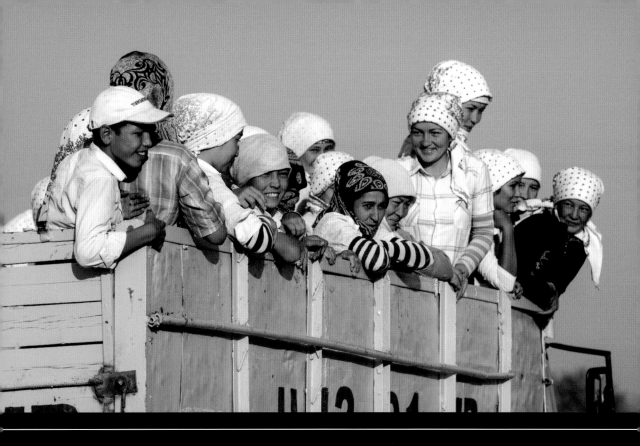

**188** Regardless of the type of goods stowed at the start, truck drivers in the informal world must deal with human cargo, which in any case will be added to the one initially loaded on and which tends to gradually increase in volume along the way.

**189** Comfort is not one of the requirements that these Uzbeki passengers evaluated at the time when they asked for passage to drivers from passing trucks. They only care about the direction, as space can always be found. Before getting out, some coins will contribute to the increased fuel consumption caused by their addition.

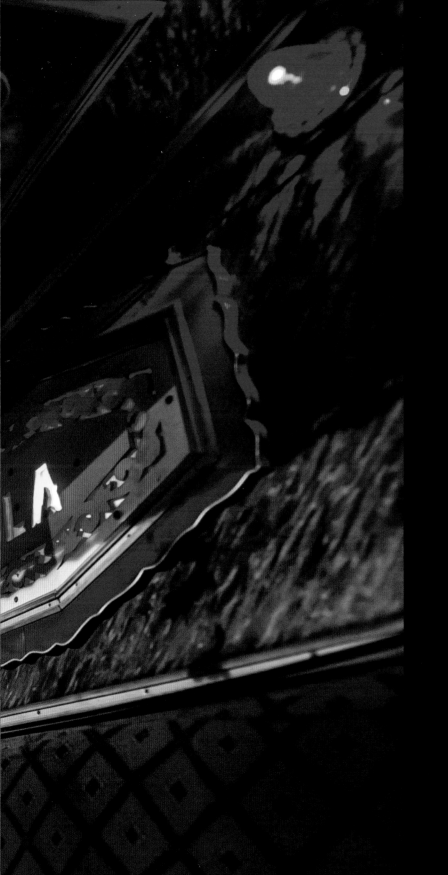

**190-191** Truck drivers are not like other carriers in India. These hard-working laborers, able to drive their vehicles for an inconceivable amount of hours, live almost in symbiosis with their vehicles, customizing them, furnishing them and making them unique.

**191** The pride of the Indian truck driver while climbing on his vehicle can also be seen from his clothing. Not only is the cab customized according to personal taste, but often even the exterior reflects the driver's identity and makes the vehicle immediately recognizable.

# With Experience

Precise and expert movements, repeated thousands, even millions, of times, that bear witness to skill, knowledge and tradition: we have photographed so many jobs pervaded with the inestimable worth of experience. This sort of magical ingredient seems to be part of an ancient secret formula, the unique product of the sum of so many errors, considerations, adjustments, tiny daily changes. Admittedly, all types of work require a certain amount of experience, but some in particular seem to rely solely upon the foundation of experience itself. These appear to be based on activities that cannot be only taught, but rather take on value when they are repeated, absorbed and lived through the knowledge of infinite movements. This may well be the spark that fascinates us most in our observation of this 'informal' work: awareness. Perhaps the very experience we attempted to photograph consists above all of awareness, that intimate satisfaction enjoyed by every person who does something 'according to the book', looking back to the past as well as forward to the future, while concentrating their movements in the present. We have seen, with our objective lens, these people at work in perfect harmony, almost a form of communion, with the space around them. Even when the work was tough, grueling and dangerous or life threatening, people were aware and self-assured regarding what was to be done, thanks to the experience they had acquired. In our modern world, this certainty and self-assurance seem to have vanished into thin air, consumed by continuous change, constant technical updating, and the unnatural speed with which all processes change. Aldous Huxley wisely stated, "Experience is not what happens to a man; it is what a man does with what happens to him." With our cameras, we have tried to capture the effects made by these occurrences, inevitably updating our own experiences.

# Drug Dealers

Forever a problem in any society, certain drugs are tolerated, commercialized, at times even managed by the State itself. Some of these substances have become part of the tradition of entire populations, inducing behaviors and habits that are extremely difficult to eradicate. Drug dealers don't always carry drugs in their pockets or whisper their prices and available quality in your ear; they sometimes even have stalls or small shops. They sit on the ground in rural markets, frequently moving to meet the needs of customers. Often Governments are complicit in their toleration of them, in legitimizing them, and provide little or no information or prevention measures. But dealers are always ready to sell a leaf, a root or powder to those who often invest most of their meager family income in smoking or swallowing their life away.

**195** Directly out of a small government run shop, a *bhang* vendor offers passers-by a ball of the famous mixture derived from cannabis. Indians consume *bhang* when they have a fever or dysentery, but especially during *holi*, the festival of colors, to feel less tired.

**196-197** An old betel nut seller prepares the slaked lime which, combined in small bite-sized doses containing a slice of betel nut wrapped in a betel-pepper leaf, helps to free the body of alkaloids and produces a mildly stimulating effect. A pinch of cinnamon gives flavor to the whole thing.

**198** From the east of Africa to Micronesia, via Pakistan, India, Southeast Asia and Papua New Guinea, betel nut consumers number in the hundreds of millions. Vendors are often accompanied by their children who, by being there, help to support the widespread belief that the use of this substance is harmless.

**199** Small shops which sell betel nuts are common throughout South-East Asia. The product is very cheap and its consumption is extremely widespread such that traders can count on a large number of occasional customers, as well as on their regulars.

**200-201** In the separatist states of northeast India, caught between
the borders of Bhutan and Myanmar, opium crops are widespread.
The proud Naga tribe, fearsome headhunters, are now dedicated more
to the consumption of this hallucinogenic substance than to war rites.

**201** In the mountainous areas of Nagaland (India), villages are
very isolated from one other. Those who provide opium to smokers
also consume it themselves in an endless spiral that over time
disintegrates the concept of authority and family.
The largest producers are the villages of Myanmar, thanks
to an almost nonexistent border between these tribes.

# Henna
# Merchants

HENNA MERCHANTS AND PRODUCERS CARRY
ON THE LEGACY OF ANCIENT TRADITIONS.
THIS SUBSTANCE HAS ALWAYS MAINLY BEEN USED
FOR AESTHETIC PURPOSES, SUCH AS HAIR COLORING
AND SKIN DECORATION FOR RITUALS. MERCHANTS
OF THIS PLANT, ALREADY BEING USED BY THE ANCIENT
EGYPTIANS, OBTAIN A FINE GREEN, YELLOW POWDER
FROM THE LEAVES AND DRIED BRANCHES, WHICH IN SOME
CULTURES IS EVEN AN IMPORTANT RITUAL WEDDING GIFT.
USING LARGE ROUND STONES FOR GRINDING,
LARGE SACKS ARE FILLED WITH THIS PRIZED BEAUTY POWDER,
WHICH THE VENDORS THEN DIVIDE INTO SMALL BAGS.
ONE ASPECT THAT SHOULD NOT BE UNDERESTIMATED
IS THE HEALING PROPERTIES OF HENNA, ABLE TO
PREVENT VARIOUS SKIN DISEASES, WHICH IN A WAY
ALSO ASSOCIATES THE MERCHANTS WITH VENDORS
OF TRADITIONAL MEDICINE.

202-203   In the East and in Mediterranean Africa, precious henna powder is used in wedding ceremonies for temporary tattoos on the hands and feet in a ceremony in India called *mehndi*. Often the vendors of this substance are also great artists and help women from all social classes create beautiful adornments.

204   In this Iranian workshop, to obtain the compact yellow-green powder known as *henna*, or as it is more often called with its French name *hennè*, the roots and the leaves of the *lawsonia inermis* shrub are dried and ground with a large millstone pulled by donkeys or driven by internal combustion engines.

204-205   In an environment kept free of moisture by numerous cast iron stoves, these men package one kilogram bags of fine henna powder and then impress the brand that attests to its Iranian origin onto the canvas, the guarantee of one of the best products in the world.

# Coin Makers

TODAY IT IS A RARE PRIVILEGE TO WITNESS COINS BEING MINTED. IN MANY OF THE COUNTRIES WE TRAVELLED
THROUGH THIS IS STILL ONE OF THE MOST REGULATED AND CONTROLLED ENVIRONMENTS. IN FACT, IT IS NO LONGER
AN ARTISAN OCCUPATION IN ANY WAY. AND YET IN RURAL AREAS ON REMOTE ISLANDS, STILL FAITHFUL TO ANCIENT TRADITIONS,
WE MET SEVERAL COIN MAKERS. WORKING THE MATERIALS BY HAND TAKES TIME, PATIENCE AND INCREDIBLE PRECISION.
BY MAKING COINS, THEY ARE PRODUCING ITEMS WITH SHARED SOCIAL VALUE, SYMBOLS OF WEALTH, A GUARANTEE
IN MARRIAGE CONTRACTS AND FOR FUNERAL RITES. IN ADDITION TO THE PATIENCE REQUIRED, ANCIENT TRADITIONAL SKILLS ARE USED,
HANDED DOWN FROM GENERATION TO GENERATION TO PRODUCE THESE TRADE ITEMS PAR EXCELLENCE.
IT IS OF NO IMPORTANCE IF, INSTEAD OF METAL ALLOY, THESE PARTICULAR COINS ARE MADE OF SHELLS.

**206** The populations of some remote Pacific islands still use shells as currency. This happens in the Solomon Islands, for example, and also in the Banks, a small island chain north of Vanuatu. In Papua New Guinea, on the other hand, large *kina* shells are still a symbol of high social status.

**208** Small shells are not used individually, but rather gathered together in long necklaces that attest to their value given primarily by the long process required to create this object. Men carefully thread a small plant twine through the hole at the center of the coins.

**208-209** After lengthy abrasion work done by the older women of the village with a kind of ingenious hand drill or simple rubbing with sand on a small mortar, only the central part of the original shell remains, perforated and extremely thinned out.

# Cattle Breeders

The pillars of cattle breeding are undoubtedly the animals and constant dedication. This occupation is well-tolerated when it involves sedentary farming, whereas semi-nomadic cattle breeding is still regarded with suspicion, in particular, for example, pastoral nomads who tend to also move their families. Yet cattle breeders have always played a key role in affirming animals as a measure of society, a source of wealth, assurance, employment opportunities, loans and gifts. In short, as well as doing an undoubtedly useful job, cattle breeders have also always been a vehicle for the flow of goods and people. Through the use and trading of animals, cattle breeders therefore simultaneously assume the roles of advocates of production and service providers.

210-211 These young shepherds follow their flocks accompanying them where the pasture is best suited to their needs. In the rugged mountains of Yemen, the younger lambs often remain trapped by rocks and have to be recovered one by one and taken back to their mothers.

212-213  In many countries of the world, it is the young people that take care of the handling of the animals at pasture, often aided by experienced dogs. At the end of the day, these young shepherds from Uzbekistan lead goats and sheep back to the house while the older men take care of the milking and shearing.

214  Often the person taking care of the animals is the same one who then arranges for the collection of the products, their processing, marketing and selling them, as in the case of milk, butter or cheese, or for wool, skins or meat.

214-215  This shepherd from the Maramures district in northern Romania has spent a lifetime with his animals, eating their meat and drinking their milk and dressing himself with their skins. They not only represent his job, but have given him his whole lifestyle and have allowed him to raise his children.

**216** In the poorest countries, the wealth of a family can also be represented by a single animal. This girl from the Bengal countryside very carefully takes care of the only cow that guarantees and ensures the existence of her entire family.

**217** In villages in the highlands of Ethiopia, animals not only represent the wealth of a family, but also the extent of their social power. In the Surma tribe, tasks are assigned according to age group. Young people take care of the herds and flocks, while adults protect the village

**218**   Sheep farming is one of the oldest forms of breeding and differs from the latter because the animals feed themselves by moving around in nature. The conflict between pastoralists and breeders is inevitable, though both trades that have always led men to nomadism or settling.

**218-219**   A strong symbiosis between animals and their shepherds is frequently established, as it is the shepherd who not only has to accompany them to where the pastures are best suited to their needs, but also to protect them from predators, prevent them from getting lost or hurt, and assist them during childbirth.

**220** Nomads are almost always also breeders. The animals are their mobile heritage and the primary source of their livelihood. In the case of camels, the animals also act as a means of transport for the breeders and for goods.

**221** Nomadic breeders are constantly moving and are not able to take advantage of weekly or monthly city markets. Therefore, they only attend the largest annual fairs that gather together thousands of animals. The town of Pushkar in Rajasthan is host to the largest camel fair in the world.

# Paddy Field
# Workers

Across the world this ancient occupation
is mainly carried out by women. They are often
laborers hired for the planting and harvesting
seasons, when there is need for more workers.
They plant or harvest the green seedlings for many
hours a day, with their legs immersed in the water
of the paddy fields, covering their entire bodies
to protect themselves against the sun and insects.
On top of the humid heat they have to work in,
they often suffer from rheumatism and malaria.
Paddy field workers still carry out their work
by hand, producing one of Asia's main food
resources; plant after plant, grain after grain.

222-223  The term rice worker originally meant the seasonal workers of the rice fields that pulled out the weeds that could compromise the growth of rice. Today, this term is extended to all processes in the rice fields, from the transfer of seedlings to the harvesting of ripe plants.

224  Transplantation by hand is still the most widely used technique in the less developed economies of Asia and Africa. This technique requires great sacrifices from workers in terms of fatigue and physical discomfort, but helps preserve the plants from aggressive weeds in agricultural areas that do not use herbicides.

225  Young rice plants, between 10 and 22 days old, are placed in the ground in groups by rice workers who always work bent over with their legs immersed in water for many hours per day. The plants need to be aligned a few centimeters from each other so as to obtain the right growth density.

# Tea
# Pickers

THIS LABORIOUS WORK IS ALSO MAINLY CARRIED OUT
BY WOMEN. BOUND TO SEASONAL AGRICULTURAL WORK,
THESE WORKERS MIGRATE AS NEEDED TO LIVE FOR MONTHS
ON THE PLANTATIONS. THE PICKERS PROTECT THEIR SKIN
FROM THE SUN WITH LARGE HATS AND CLOTHING
THAT IS AT TIMES EXTREMELY COLORFUL, EVERY NOW
AND THEN SINGING IN UNISON. THEY FACE MANY HOURS
OF HARD WORK, BENT OVER THE PLANTS OR LEAVES
AND MANEUVERING DEFTLY EVEN AT HIGH ALTITUDES.
THEY PICK TEA LEAVES, A RAW MATERIAL THAT IS
A MAINSTAY OF THEIR COUNTRIES' TRADITIONAL DIETS,
AS WELL AS A PRODUCT OF FUNDAMENTAL IMPORTANCE
FOR INTERNATIONAL EXPORTS. AT THE SAME TIME,
THESE WORKERS GUARANTEE VALUABLE SUPPORT
FOR THEIR FAMILIES.

226-227 The largest tea producing region in the world is located in the territories of northeast India in Assam. This inaccessible region provides 55% of India's tea crop and provides 31% of this product to the world markets. The entire harvest is done by hand.

228-229 The collection of the tasty leaves is entrusted entirely to women, who must distinguish and gently tear off only the leaves ready to be processed. Men present on the plantations have only a monitoring and inspection role.

**230-231**  More than 800 landowners provide thousands of women with constant work in the tea plantations of Assam. Women protect themselves from the scorching sun with hats similar to those used by rice workers but, in contrast, they do not need to stay immersed in water in order to work.

**232** There are large tea plantations in southern China, with the regions of Guangxi, Sichuan, Hunan and Yunnan producing very particular highly sought-after leaves. The special *pu'er* tea is cultivated in the Yunnan area, a tea very popular for its smooth earthy taste.

**232-233** *Pu'er* tea undergoes a very particular treatment: the leaves are ground and pulverized and the paste that is obtained is pressed into a mold to obtain a tile. In this way, the tea can be easily transported and it is therefore much appreciated by nomadic populations.

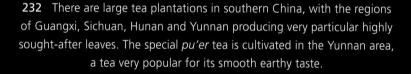

# With Creativity

## chapter 8

The most imaginative and unusual component of this category of informal work is the result of our adaptation to the environment. Thanks to the great energy generated by creativity, we have seen people overcome barriers, conceive new meanings, lend a different meaning to life and even contribute to spirituality and what is sacred. In short, this human creativity succeeds in inventing concepts which become real and sees relationships where they didn't seem to exist, and generates opportunities even when this appears to be impossible. What do street artists, snake charmers and sculptors have in common? Perhaps, above all, a personal, authentic approach to life, hand in hand with a touch of madness that induces them to follow paths that others often refuse to consider. Then there is the unquestionable magic of their extreme vulnerability and their acceptance of their fragile condition, which triggers creativity, innovation and change in the form of ideas, which must then be put into practice without the comfort of social approval. This special type of work, which, fortunately, is to be found everywhere – albeit expressed through different modalities and in different social contexts – is always a precious resource for society. In fact, it is thanks to creativity that initiative, the essence of all occupations, takes shape in the most clear-cut and precise way, thereby demonstrating that the secret lies not so much in the final product but rather in the process that leads people's minds along this path. And so, in the dust of an improvised courtyard workshop, breathing the muggy air in a circus tent set up in a street or under the weak light of old glow lamps, we have seen the results of the creativity and imagination of so many men and women throughout the world. We have captured their dreams – often tempered with their ironic judgment of themselves – their dogged commitment, their irrepressible enthusiasm. And, we have captured the subtle fragrance of a form of work that, at times, succeeds in transforming an idea into a new occupation.

# Street
# Artists

STREET ARTISTS LIVE THEIR LIVES IN AN EXTREMELY
PARTICULAR WORK CONTEXT, APART FROM RARE CASES
OF ATTEMPTS TO BECOME INSTITUTIONALIZED.
BUT WHEREAS IN THE REGULATED WORLD THEY NEED
SOME KIND OF AUTHORIZATION, A SPECIAL PERMIT
TO MOVE AMONG THE FOLDS OF THE SYSTEM,
IN THE INFORMAL WORLD THEIR STATUS AS ARTISTS
DOES NOT NEED OFFICIAL RECOGNITION, AS SPIRITUAL,
AT TIMES ALMOST MAGICAL RECOGNITION IS SUFFICIENT.
NOMADS, MESTIZOS, CULTURALLY CONTAMINATED,
THEY IMPROVISE THEIR THEATERS AND WORKING CONTEXTS.
THEY CELEBRATE TRADITION, EXPRESS VALUES AND LIVE
IRREGULARLY BY SHARED COMMON RULES.
AND YET THEY KEEP THE CREATIVITY OF THE PEOPLE
ALIVE, ACTING OUT LIFE ITSELF BY OFFERING
ENTERTAINMENT TO EVEN THE LOWEST SOCIAL CLASSES.
EVERY ENCOUNTER WE HAD WITH THE STREET ART WORLD
OPENED DOORS FOR US, CREATING CONTACTS
AND SPECIAL RELATIONSHIPS, BUILDING BRIDGES.
WITH THEIR CREATIVITY, THESE ARTISTS CONTINUOUSLY
CONFIRM THEIR EXISTENCE OUTSIDE THE SHARED SYSTEM.

**236-237** The unmistakable silhouette of a colorful tent attracted us, pushing us to find out which circus company had gone into the mudflats of Sunderbans in Bangladesh, the swamp into which the river Ganges drains.

**238-239** One of the principal attractions of the "Great Royal Bengal Circus", the tightrope walking goat Amita, immediately won the hearts of all twelve spectators, including us, who certainly did not spare praise and applause.

**239** In a real circus, versatility is key. The "great Kalidas" for example, who amazingly took our tickets at the entrance, also performs hovering in the sky like a trapeze artist, as the tamer of a group of turkeys and, surprisingly, even turns into a miniature tightrope walker.

**240-241** Artists from around the world are well aware that, when accompanied by darkness, fire fascinates the audience like nothing else. And when fire comes out of a mouth and is spewed into the sky, the imagination of everyone jumps to legendary dragons and they spontaneously applaud.

**241** Just a few meters from the waves of the Pacific Ocean, these fire-eaters from Tonga island manage to hold their breath for a fairly diverse audience, also including Marines from an American aircraft carrier in port.

242  Defying danger, putting their lives at stake, and playing on the most ancient fears of people has always been an inspiration for street artists in every country in the world. Some coins are enough to turn ancient wisdom into a job.

243  As much as in India a meeting with a cobra is a frequent occurrence, often on the streets of the city, those who manage to enchant the most deadly snakes are able at the same time to enchant the public, who for millennia have economically honored and rewarded men who are respected by the "king of the reptiles."

MUSICIANS ARE PERHAPS CONSIDERED ARTISTS PAR EXCELLENCE BY EVERYONE, ALTHOUGH THIS RARELY INCLUDES THE ONES WE HEAR IN THE STREETS OF THE WORLD, THE BACKGROUND MUSIC TO OUR STEPS, DEVOTING THEMSELVES ENTIRELY TO THIS ONE PROFESSION. AND YET THEY ARE ALMOST ALWAYS CARRYING ON A FAMILY TRADITION, TRUE CREATORS WHO ARE PASSIONATE ABOUT SOUNDS AND MUSIC, IMPORTANT AT ALL LEVELS OF SOCIETY. THEY MAKE THEIR LIVING BY PLAYING AT RELIGIOUS CEREMONIES, PARTIES, WEDDINGS, IN SHORT, CELEBRATING BOTH LIFE AND DEATH. FOR IMPORTANT EVENTS, EVEN THE POOREST PEOPLE WILL FIND A WAY TO PAY FOR THEIR PRESENCE. SOMETIMES THE CREATIVITY OF INDIVIDUALS AND THE EVOLUTION OF TRADITIONS LEAD THEM TO INVENT AND USE NEW MUSICAL INSTRUMENTS, WHICH NEVERTHELESS INEVITABLY BECOME PART OF A POPULATION'S DNA.

**245** On the streets of Cuba, it is easy to meet musicians who move from place to place carrying their instruments. Music is part of the DNA of the Cubans and the pay for musicians is never very high considering that people can hear music for free almost anywhere.

**246** Mandu is an enchanted place and almost unknown in Indian tourism. The ancient architecture of the temples covered in vegetation creates spectacular acoustics, worthy of the best theaters.
The players of the *bansoori* know how to exploit it, offering moments suspended in time for just a few coins.

**247** We often cross the deserts of Rajasthan to reach the magical city of Jaisalmer. At the foot of its bastions is a delicate pool of water surrounded by ancient temples. Each time, sitting on the white steps, an old *surbahar* player is waiting for us, as motionless as the time that inhabits these places.

**248-249** Music is normally made to enchant, move, and entertain those who hear it. But during *voodoo* rites, musicians perform an exhausting involving act, contributing with obsessive hallucinatory rhythms to the state of trance of the worshipping officials.

**250**  To play this gigantic Pan flute, which generates the ultra-low sounds necessary to support the incessant rhythm of very special songs, it takes years of training. This musician has to vibrate the column of air contained in the large piece bamboo by using only the breath of his lungs.

**250-251**  This group of musicians from the Solomon Islands voluntarily performs on various islands for a small fee. The members of the group have composed the music and also built all the instruments used with the necessary supports.

**252-253** In the charming bays of lost Gaua, a small island which belongs to the Banks island chain, to the north of the Vanuatu islands located at the center of the Pacific Ocean, you can watch a musical show that is unique in all the world: the *water dance*.

**253** The women of this unusual group have developed a very special technique: they use the ocean water as instruments, striking its surface with their hands, stirring it and making it fall to extract sounds and truly captivating rhythms.

# Statue
# Makers

Sculptors of the sacred, skilled manipulators of not always noble materials, creators of shapes that are instantly recognizable, statue makers are always busy in the various and long stages of craftsmanship. Drawn together for convenience in dedicated neighborhoods, they produce idols for religious temples and festivals, as well as statues to sell to individuals. Often groups of artisans work together on one large piece, perfecting, painting, completing it thanks to precise teamwork. Sometimes, however, it can be a long, individual process. Raw clay and straw replace the marble and stone of the past, often so that the pieces can dissolve in sacred rivers. This is because sometimes the statues created by these special sculptors are a kind of mandala that will be destroyed, shortly after it is finished, at the height of some religious event.

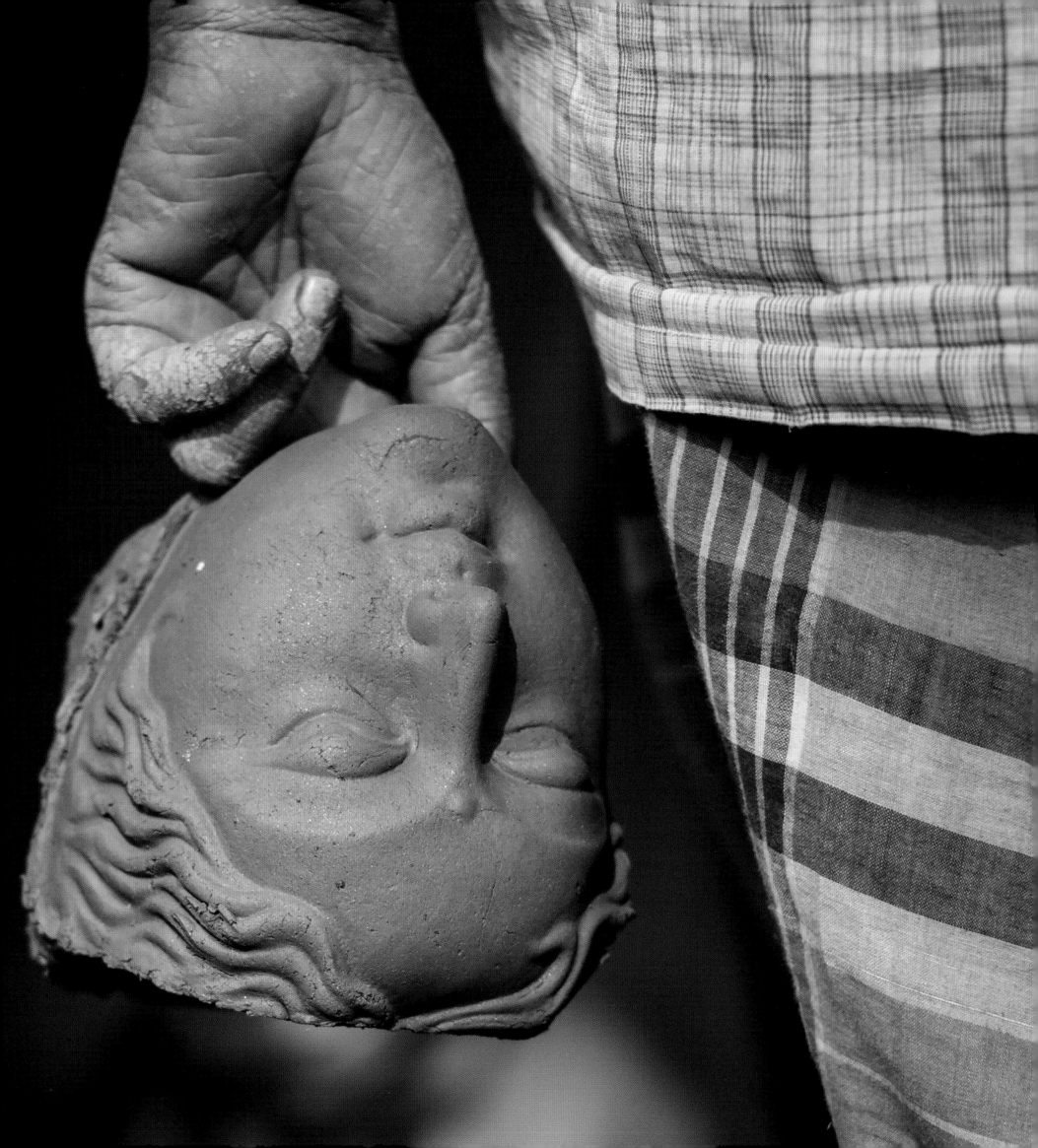

254-255   In the heart of big, chaotic Kolkata stretches out Kumartuli, a neighborhood where the incessant bustling of work never ceases. Thousands of craftsmen, artists, truck drivers, workers, and vendors create, produce and trade statues and religious effigies for the whole country.

256   Operators in this industry are highly specialized, especially those that contribute to the creation of large statues. Some workshops produce only parts of the whole figures and the reproductions of faces and divine expressions are entrusted to the most expert.

257   Even the craftsmen that shape the hands and feet of the statues are chosen from the best as it is always these parts of the body that create problems for artists all over the world. Hands and feet, precious and delicate, are therefore applied only at the end of the creation process.

**258-259** In the endless workshops of Kumartuli, thousands of different religious images are created from almost nothing by using mud, clay and a coating of straw supported by iron wires and small wooden stakes. Thanks to improvised scaffolding, groups of sculptors are able to work simultaneously.

**259** When the work is finished and the material that it is made of has dried completely, the statues are brought to the painters, whose job it is to give the effigies the colors set out in the ancient scriptures, unchanged for thousands of years just as the shapes, accessories and positions of the gods.

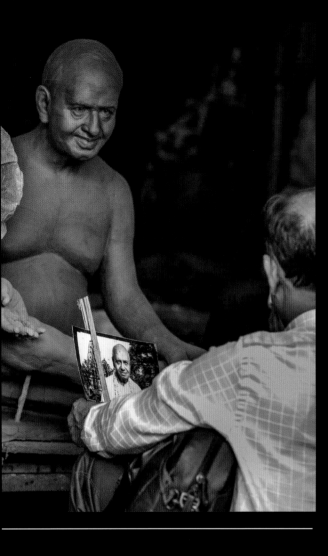

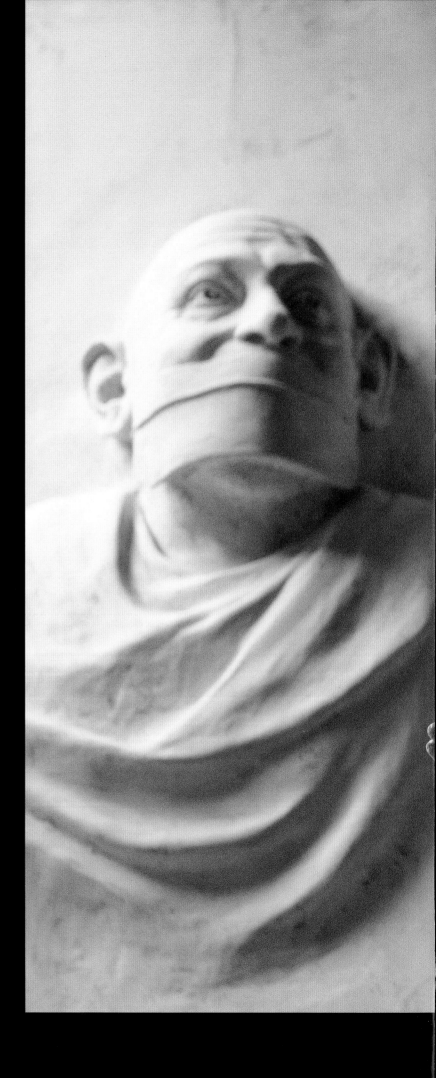

**260** Kumartuli not only produces sacred works but occasionally also secular objects. Sometimes a rich family commissions the statue of a relative who has gone on to a better life or an institution wishes to finance the statuary image of a well-deserving member of the community. In this case, a photograph is used to create the likeness.

**260-261** This man, who is working on a piece that features three major figures from Jainism, is experienced in the technique of bas-relief and works alone in his shop. To make his representations smooth, he uses an abrasive paste that he spreads for hours with his bare hands until the pain forces him to stop.

# WINDOWS TO THE WORLD

Windows are extremely malleable elements. They can cut off the outside world just as they can open up to it. But these windows, the inspiration behind the now diffused concept of *Windows*, which generated a new and shared revolution in the way we think, open up a series of snapshots of the world, patiently identified, photographed and cataloged. Our small collections of images are designed to offer a different way of seeing the countries we visited, a point of view that starts off with micro details, followed by close-ups and arriving at macro shots, the whole picture. Because sometimes starting with a small detail can help you get to the heart of the matter. For this reason, we left a few small windows open on the world, as they are also testimony to how man daily lives his work. Leaving the concept of *doing* aside momentarily, we have collected little things, different forms, objects that still lead to human operativeness without going through the front door, taking advantage of a small window left open at the back.

# SLACKERS

Idleness has always been the flip side of work's coin and attests to a different use of time, nevertheless influenced by cultural factors. There are slackers in every corner of the world; they evade the rules, whether formal or informal; rules that would have them employed, focused, busy. Contrariwise, they seem to take possession of a vital rhythm of life, one that is more intimately human, robbing the system of a moment to sleep, a space in which to daydream, a little extra time in life to casually watch the rest of the world getting worked up about producing something. Far from being part of the privileged elite which thanks to their status can avoid working, slackers can also materialize in social environments with the greatest economic and social hardship. Sometimes just temporarily disconnected from the system, they nevertheless remind us that in addition to objective time, spent obsessing about modern world efficiency, there is also subjective time, which remains the sole and exclusive property of every man and woman.

# SIGNS

Forever signs have served to capture our attention, as faithful representations of a business's activities or of a social idea connected to an occupation, a profession or a job. Our images portray them defining the physical boundaries of stores, decorating their walls, describing tradition, religion, common feelings, or simply celebrating personal experience autobiographically. Always in the eye-line of the observer-passersby, often framing doors or windows, in many countries they represent a true expression of pop-art and they can be seen as an extremely interesting product of historical and cultural processes. All over the world, signs replace absent windows, emphasize otherwise insignificant places, adding color and decorating gray and dusty areas, yet always in some way celebrating work, skill, competence. They are nevertheless testimonies, synthetic products, functional focal points.

# TOOLS

Hands were once man's tool par excellence. They were able to choose, move, hold, work on matter to transform it. The first manifestation of human intelligence, hands, from which all tools are descended, evolve and become the engine of each and every tool, the driving force that handles and uses specific objects. Using a tool brings to life projects that man first conceives in theory and then seeks to effectively reproduce. Tools therefore represent the fundamental entrance of technology into work and activities. They have always made achieving objectives easier, possible, accelerating, simplifying and improving man's work. They are bodily extensions that are able to reach places our hands can't. A manifestation of evolution, historical testimonies, cultural products; tools have always been the means par excellence used by man to change matter and the world.

# IAGO AND GRETA

Looking at your images when get back from a trip is like taking a different route, choosing to go down a different path at a junction. Perhaps, once you have assimilated them, you may even question their actual purpose, and the circle closes just by looking once more at all the frames that have frozen cells and preserved atoms in time. Among these images, which have the miraculous power of leading us to embark on a new journey, we are particularly attached to the ones taken "behind the scenes." Historically considered less noble, judged separately and usually relegated to separate storage folders, behind-the-scenes photos are active witnesses to events, synergies and modalities. They are practical maps and ex-votos of emotionally charged experiences. We always treat them with great care, not as trophies or proof of evidence, but rather as post-cards immortalized with micro details. The size of one of our smiles, a subject in the background oblivious to being part of the picture, elements in the landscape that our memory has no recollection of, objects that are unwitting witnesses to an event. In short, in our opinion behind-the-scenes photos do not deserve the marginal treatment they often receive, especially if taken with love. We are always affected by them because we inevitably recall a state of mind, a critical moment, an overcome obstacle, or simply an exchanged look while sharing a moment. "Behind the scenes" is therefore the journey in its essence, and basically everything else comes second.

In a small village in southern China, an ingenious craftsman makes a living by cleverly carving
small blocks of wax into the features of his customers.

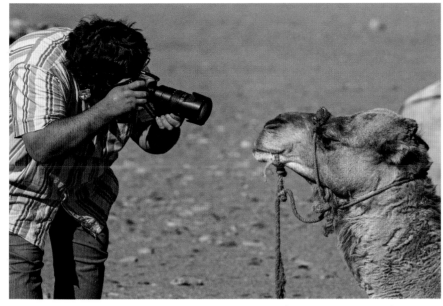

The nomads of the desert are expert breeders of camels and dromedaries and practically live in symbiosis with their animals.

Young monks studying at the Bagaya Kyaung monastery on Ava island (Myanmar) are not distracted even a moment in the event of an unexpected visit.

Along the dusty roads of Uzbekistan, classic means of transport are often replaced by large trucks whose containers overflow with silent disciplined passengers.

In rural communities in Togo, the huts used as schools are always built in the middle of nowhere so that they are equidistant from and offer services to at least three or four villages.

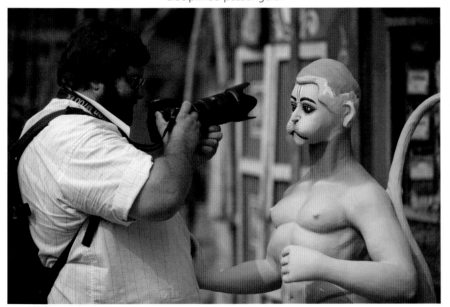

Kumartuli is the Kolkata neighborhood where most of the Bengal religious are created, assembled and shaped, both for use in temples and private homes.

Those who understand India know that contact between people is the indispensable key to enter this magical country which jealously guards a great treasure of humanity.

**Iago Corazza**, journalist and filmmaker, but above all a photographer and traveler, got his start at 15 years old working with a major photography agency from Bologna. His passion for travel led him to Africa first as a traveler and then as a tour guide across the continent. He has made documentaries and photo features in 120 countries around the world and as a director and cinematographer, he has worked on programs for the most important Italian and foreign broadcasters, such as CNN and Turner Classic Movies. Corazza has been awarded three Telegatti awards in Italy and the prestigious Telly Award for culture in the United States. He led an expedition of two Jeeps from Bologna to Miami (Florida) taking five months and crossing 64,000 kilometers. He is in charge of the production of cultural performances, shows, and musical events televised on various national broadcasters. He is responsible for the anthropological section of the magazine "Oasis" and has dozens of editorial publications with a variety of newspapers and publishing houses to his credit. Among these is White Star Publishers, which has produced significant anthropological monographs including "New Guinea. The Last Men", "Japan. Light and shadows in the Land of the Rising Sun" and "This is My Home. Journey through the Evolution of Human Dwellings." Corazza is an advocate and collaborator with UNICEF. (www.iago.com)

**Greta Ropa** is a writer and a correspondent in foreign languages. She graduated with a degree in Education and Human Resources, and she has years of experience in the fashion and advertising industry to her credit. She works both as a model and photographic model for numerous companies of national and international importance. Passionate about travel and photography, she has made documentaries in more than 100 countries worldwide. In 2002, along with Iago Corazza, she participated as a photographer in the expedition by Jeep from Bologna to Miami. Ropa works for film and television, and collaborates as a writer with various magazines and publishing houses such as "Oasis" and White Star Publishers, for whom she published, together with Iago Corazza, three important anthropological monographs.

**Thanks to...**

*... those who guided us through our adventures:*

Anand Shripat, Alessandra Della Morte, Catalin Pascanu, Daniel Wakra, Dorji Tsedan, Edvinas Pundys, Idriss Amrani, Karo Serobyan, Keti Tevzadze, Paul K. Akakpo, Raffaele Montagna, Raj Kumar "Prince" Nanda, Sanjeev Chandra, Srikant Mishra, Vinay Jaiswal, Zahara Anvar, Joaquim Bezerra de Araujo, Zhao Fan Cao

*... those who supported us during the writing of this book:*

Giordano Gardenghi, Lorenzo Quintarelli, Luca Poggi, Marco Mercuri, Manuela Paoletti, Matteo Benetti, Rino and Carloalberto Canobbi, L'Operosa srl, Paolo and Paolofilippo Nugari, Roberto Falsini, Vittorio Kulczycki

*... and to all our travel companions that shared these experiences with us.*

WHITE STAR PUBLISHERS

WS White Star Publishers® is a registered trademark
property of White Star s.r.l.

© 2016 White Star s.r.l.
Piazzale Luigi Cadorna, 6 - 20123 Milan, Italy
www.whitestar.it

Translation and Editing: Richard Pierce and TperTradurre s.r.l.

ISBN 978-88-544-1088-6
1 2 3 4 5 6    20 19 18 17 16

Printed in Croatia